THE AAU BASKETBALL BIBLE

EVERYTHING YOU'D BETTER KNOW ABOUT YOUTH BASKETBALL AND COLLEGE RECRUITING

TROY HORNE

Copyright © 2020 by Buggily Group Inc. All Right Reserved.

Listen To Tthe #1 Youth Basketball PodcastShow That Inspired the book at:

http://hoopchalk.com/

The AAU Basketball Bible
Everything You'd Better Know About AAU Basketball

The AAU Basketball Bible
Everything You'd Better Know About AAU Basketball

Table Of Contents

WHY I WROTE THIS BOOK

I wrote this book because I didn't want parents like me to feel helpless while navigating their way through the world of AAU. I was one of those lost parents when I started out. I have a kid who wants to play basketball at the college and eventually the pro level and I didn't know a thing about the process. I have a kid who has NBA dreams. I have a kid who was entering into a world that I knew nothing about and I wanted to learn everything that I could to help him get to where he wanted to go.

I wrote this book for the thousands if not millions of parents who would otherwise struggle or be led down the wrong path. This book is for parents who might otherwise spend countless hours and thousands of dollars pursuing or working on the wrong things only to find that their kid's basketball journey ends with high school when it didn't have to.

I wrote this book for the newby basketball parents who are coming behind me. I was once in your shoes and I know that the information that you will read in this book will shave off years of bad advice and save you thousands of dollars. I wrote this book for you. I hope that you will use this book as a resource as you continue or begin your basketball journey with your family. See you all in the gym! – Troy Horne (aka Moses' Dad)

WHY YOU SHOULD READ THIS BOOK

This book will help you understand the new world of AAU basketball. Imagine being able to ask over 40 basketball college coaches, NBA Vets, High School Basketball prep school coaches and ESPN ranked players what they would do if they had it to do all over again. Imagine being able to get advice from NBA champions, trainers and Euroleague players. Well that is what we did and we put it all in this book.

There isn't another resource in the world like this one and I'm grateful to be a little part of why you have a chance to hold it in the palm of your hand. This is the first book of its kind and you have a chance to learn things that other parents wish that they would have known during their child's basketball journey. You have a chance to hear from D1 coaches how to get recruited. You have a chance to hear from EYBL coaches how to work towards your goal of playing in college. You get to hear from NBA vets how they took their career from unknown high school or college player to the NBA! You get to hear it all!

The AAU Basketball Bible
Everything You'd Better Know About AAU Basketball

Read this book and apply all of the knowledge that they share to your journey. The information alone will put you miles ahead of your peers. So sit back. Take out a pencil and paper and get ready to take your game to the next level. See you on the other side.

If you want to go even deeper and get literally EVERYTHING that we did to help Moses

- Play Varsity as a freshman on one of the top 5 High School teams in the state.

- Learn on court mental toughness

- Maximize his growth potential.

- Improve his nutrition and…

- Work to prevent injury head on over to…

http://aaubasketballbible.com/

Over there we give you EVERYTHING!

CHAPTER 1. "YOU MIGHT WANT TO GET HIM INTO BASKETBALL..."

It was a regular day after school. I don't remember the exact day, but I like to call it "the day that will live in infamy." I will never forget it. This day was going to be the day that changed the course of our lives and our pocketbooks forever. It was a field day at our son's school, and we were doing the regular watch-your-kid–do-tug-of-war-and–throw-water-balloons thang. Ms. Judy, a small, but strong spirited New Yorker and Moses' P.E. teacher, approached me. Ms. Judy was awesome. Her spirit and her accent was like a breath of fresh air for this former Broadway performer turned entrepreneurial dad who was now living in Denver, which kind of felt like moving to the sticks at the time.

She walked up to me, and in true East Coast fashion she looked me straight in the eye and asked, "Are you Moses' Dad?"

I paused for a moment because Ms. Judy was a force, and it took a moment to switch back into East Coast mode from country outback mode. "Yes I am." I responded.

Still staring piercingly right into my eyes, she said, "You might want to get him into basketball. He seems to have an aptitude for it."

The AAU Basketball Bible
Everything You'd Better Know About AAU Basketball

That came out of nowhere for me. Being a musician, I thought to myself *this kid is going to be a pop icon*. He was in singing lessons and piano lessons at the time. We were even driving him across town to be in the local kids performing choir. Basketball was nowhere on the radar before that day, and little did we know that after that day, basketball would be the only blip on the radar screen. The biggest blip on the sonar came out of nowhere, like a surprise iceberg to our Titanic.

After the field day, my wife Elizabeth and I went back to work on our acting school business and didn't ŧ think too much about what Ms. Judy had said. That was until the afternoon at car line pick up. As Moses hopped in the car, what Ms. Judy said hopped back into my mind. I turned to Moses, as he was putting down his backpack and fixing his seatbelt. I think that I said something like, "Hey, Ms. Judy said that you like basketball." I was totally expecting the usual unemotional kid response like, "Yeah." But instead I got flood of emotion. I can't tell you exactly what he said, but I remember thinking to myself *this is how I feel about music!*

After I listened to story after story about how he was the "3rd grade gym class hero of basketball" on our ride home and how he had swished his first shot ever, "Nothing but net," were his words, my mind switched from proud papa elation to panic. I didn't know ANYTHING about basketball. I had tried out for the team once when I was in middle school, but wasn't very good and didn't really like it. So, I quit before the tryouts were over. Needless to say, in my mind, I was not the guy to help him pursue his passion. (At that moment) Then, of course, came the flood of doubting Thomas-like quotes that I had heard about sports and basketball specifically when I was a kid. I remembered hearing people tell my little sister the same thoughts because she wanted to be a professional basketball player.

They said things like, "Do you know the odds of becoming a basketball player?" and "What if you don't grow? There were more comments like, "You have to be tall to play basketball," and "They don't even have a professional league for female basketball players." (This was pre-WNBA days.) So, all of those childhood conversations about impossibility came flooding back to me, as if someone had opened up the floodgates of the teacher-like-comments of, "You have to be realistic" and "Get a Job." Then, just as quickly as the panic had set in, it was beaten back by the adult Troy.

You see, the seven-year-old Troy was still hiding in there afraid, but the adult Troy came to his defense. The adult Troy said "Hey, they said the same things about you wanting to become a professional musician. They said that you should have a fallback plan. They said that the odds were against you ever becoming a professional musician, and they said that you would never make it, but you did.

The AAU Basketball Bible
Everything You'd Better Know About AAU Basketball

You became a professional musician and you even starred on Broadway. You have been on "Star Search," NBC's The Sing-Off, and you have toured the country as a signed recording artist; you have toured the world as a professional a cappella singer, and you made more money doing music than most people make doing a "realistic" job. You started a business in the middle of a recession because you wanted to help people reach their dreams, and you and your wife grew it to one of the largest acting schools in the state of Colorado. Tell those doubting voices to shut up!"

So, then I said to myself *well, what would you do if you were raising a professional singer?* I thought about it for a moment and then that adult Troy voice answered. "Well, take the same steps with Moses and apply them to basketball. I knew how hard it was to make it as a musician, but I also knew that there were some clear steps that I took either accidentally or on purpose that made my success possible. All I had to do was reverse engineer those steps and apply them to his love, the love of basketball, and the dream of becoming a professional NBA player.

But, before I did that, I had to know if this kid was really all in or just infatuated with being a gym class hero. Either one was cool. I just needed to know before I went all "we're going pro" on my 8-year-old. Step one: mom.

That evening, as we were getting ready for bed, I casually mentioned to my wife Elizabeth what Ms. Judy had said to me and the reaction that Moses gave me on the ride home. She said, "Basketball huh? That's different," or something like that. We were both a little fascinated and bewildered by the whole thing. Neither of us were your high school jock type. We were your musical theatre/choir nerd type. The thought of raising a jock was quite foreign to us, but we were up for the challenge. After all, this was our kid that we are talking about here.

"So, what does that mean?" she asked.

"I don't know-," I responded, "but I think that I am going to look into it for him and find out." "Sounds good," she responded.

Mom – Check.

CAN I WEAR #8 LIKE KOBE?

The next step was to determine the level of interest from the kid. The kid probably had no clue about what commitment meant past being committed to asking about ice cream and how long he could play his Nintendo DS. I had heard the stories of Tiger Woods and Venus and Serena Williams, so I knew that if this was going to happen, it would have to be parent led; but, before I got into the whole "we have to practice every day" talk, I wanted to see if he really loved this thing called basketball like he said he did. So, I sat him down and had a short talk with him that went something like this-:

"Hey, Moses." – Me

"Yes, Dad." – Moses

"What do you think about this basketball thing?" – Me

"I love it!" - Moses

"You want to play on a team?" – Me

"Sure! That would be awesome! Can I have #8 like Kobe Bryant?" – Moses

"Well, we have to tryout first. I just wanted to see if you would like to tryout and play on a team." – Me

"Yeah, dad! I would love it!" – Moses

"Cool. I will see what's out there." – Me

I am pretty sure that he went back to the playground and played with his brother and sister, or something like that, and I went straight to Google in search of basketball tryouts. Even though he had verbally committed to the team thing, I knew that making a profession out of this passion would take a lot more than that, but it was a good first step from him.

That summer he played his first season at the Y, and the look on his face after every game screamed that he was definitely all in. He was in love and I was in over my head or so I felt. That is when adult Troy chimed in again and said, "Bruh! BRUH!! You did the impossible. It ain't that hard. Do the research and figure it out! Get to work, dude!"

However, I still wasn't convinced that this wasn't just a passing phase. After all he was 8, and he was really good at singing, as expected. Maybe I should just let him play in the summer and go back to our original plan of making the next pop icon. I could have done that, but that would have been my dream and not his. So, before we went all "Richard Williams" on his butt, I decided to have the talk to end all talks with him. I sat him down again. The conversation went something like this:

"Hey, Mo." Me

"Yes, Dad." – Moses

"Do you think that you would want to be in the NBA someday?" – Me

"YES! I would LOVE that!" – Moses

"Well, it's going to take a lot of work. You are going to have to work when you don't want to. Are you up for that?" – Me

"YES!" – Moses

"Are you sure?" – Me

"YES! This is what I want to do!" – Moses

"Ok. Well, we'll give it a shot. We are going to tryout for a competitive team next season and those kids are good. If you want to make that team, you are going to have to wake me up before school and we are going to have to go to the gym and practice. Are you up for that?" – Me

"YES!" – Moses

"Ok. So, here is how this is going to go. You have to set an alarm and wake me up in the mornings. I am not going to wake you up. We have to go the gym at 5 in order to practice and get back in time for school. If you don't wake me up, we are not going, and if you miss more than two days in a row, we are not going to do it anymore. We can just play at the Y and have fun. I will support you, but you are going to have to take the first steps. Cool?" – Me

"Yup! Can you show me how to set my alarm?" – Moses

Needless to say, he woke me up every day for a week. I had bitten off more than I could chew. I was exhausted. So, I said, "Hey buddy, you have proven that you are all in, so let's just do Monday, Wednesday and Friday. That way you can get some sleep. You need your rest to grow," I told him. The truth was that I needed my rest to be sane!

A season or two went by. We hired trainers with money that we didn't have, and he and I worked out ourselves to supplement their instruction. He made team after team, we were on our way, and then it happened. He didn't make a team that he tried out for. What?! He was crushed and I was, too. However, I knew the amount of failure that came with success. So, after we got the news, I took him out for some ice cream and we talked about what happened.

"So, buddy. Are you still all in?" I asked.

"Yes." He responded. "Well, you just found out the work that we were doing wasn't enough and that's ok. You're 9-years-old. However, we have to really take a look at what we are doing and decide if you want to do more because apparently we have to do more to make it to where you want to go. Are you up for that?" I remember asking him.

I also remember him responding with a resounding "YES! I want to work hard and one day crush those guys." So, we dug in, but I made one final deal with him to test his resolve. I guess all of the testing was done because I wanted to make doubly sure that he was up for the road that lay ahead. Keep in mind that we were now financially buying in and we weren't successful business owners yet. So this was a financial stretch to say the least. I had to do my due diligence and believe you me, I did.

CHAPTER 2. THE BIG TEST

I don't know where I came up with the idea. Maybe it was all of the personal development books that I had read about how it takes 21 days to create a habit or something, but I devised a plan that I thought would be a good test of commitment. Here is how it went. Feel free to use it for your situation if it resonates with you.

Rule #1: If we start, we are going to work on this as if it is our job. Your job is now to become a professional basketball player. You will work on it at least a little every day. That means either watching videos, reading a book on the sport, or going to the gym and doing the physical work, but every day is a workday until you make it to the NBA.

Rule #2: We will do this for a full-year nonstop. After the year, you can choose to stop and not pursue this anymore. However, should you choose to continue after the year, you can't stop until you reach 18. You can take time off to rest and recoup physically or mentally. A week at a time at the most, but after that year, you are all in if you agree to continue.

Rule #3: You are not allowed to talk to anyone adult or otherwise about the "realistic possibilities" of becoming a pro. You will not be disrespectful if approached or brought into a dream doubting conversation, but inside your mind, you will be repeating the word "cancel" until they are finished talking. Your response to their questions will be a respectful, "Yes, Ma'am/Sir" or "No, Sir/Ma'am" or "I don't know; can you ask my dad/mom, sir/ma'am," or "I will have to talk to my dad/mom about that, ma'am/sir",and always say thank you.

We talked it about it over and over and over again during the year. During the year, we also asked if he wanted to quit. I even said, "Hey, we don't have to wait the whole year. If you want to quit, you can quit now." However, he never wavered. At the end of the year, he re-upped for the next 10 and our journey began. Now, the work was on me.

MY TURN TO STEP UP

I started reading blogs, books, forums, and taking him to basketball camps. I watched documentary after documentary and talked to coach after coach; he started killing it on the court. He made a name for himself in the world of Colorado basketball, and even did so outside of Colorado, winning basketball camp championship after basketball camp championship. On one specific visit to the famous Oak Hill Academy in Mouth of Wilson, VA, he even attracted the attention of one coach, Steve Smith, who caught wind of this kid after he made 7 straight 3s in a camp scrimmage. Coach Steve came to his game and did the announcing in which he referred to Moses as "Mose Curry." The work, both physical and mental, had paid off.

Moses At Oak Hill Basketball Camp

Now Moses makes every team, AAU and otherwise, that he tries out for! Let me say that again! He makes every team that he tries out for. We tested this theory during the 2018 basketball season. He tried out for five teams and made all five. He even got to crush the team that he didn't make, back when he was 8 years old. As things progressed, I continued to do the research. I continued to look for the next step. Not the step to the pros, but the next step in his career. I began to look into how to be successful in high school basketball, how to be successful in college basketball, and finally how to be successful as a pro.

We started a podcast to share this information and asked all of the questions that we thought would help us and parents like us on their journey, and suddenly the path to a successful high school career, college career, and professional athlete career began to show itself. I had a theory that it existed in the beginning, but you can imagine my surprise when like the road to El Dorado, the path suddenly started to appear. Much like the road to becoming a professional musician, it was hidden in plain sight. It was hidden, but it was there! I repeat: It…IS…there!

So what did I do? Well, first I started getting texts and calls from parents that had either listened to the podcast or knew us personally. I found that they were asking some of the same questions. There were so many questions that I started sending out formatted emails. I would just send to them the email that fit best based on their inquiries. Then, I realized that if I wrote this stuff down in a book, I could help more parents like myself who were clueless to this whole AAU basketball thing. I realized through countless conversations and podcast interviews that we had become the parents we had been looking for.

I realized that if you are willing to follow the path and make adjustments based on your specific situation, the path can be walked by anyone with the desire to have what lies at its end. The question is not will you make it; the question is, "Are you willing to take ALL of the steps and take ALL of the actions that the path will require of you?" The path asks different things from each traveler, but if your answer is "yes," you can reach the end of the yellow brick road and grab onto your dream.

If you are like me and had or have no clue about this basketball world, read on. This is about to be a deep look into everything that you had better know before you start your AAU journey. To my past self, parent with no clue, you are in luck! I have found some of the answers to the questions that you have been looking for. I wrote them down in this book. So sit down and buckle up; the ride is wild and it's about to begin.

CHAPTER 3. TRUST THE PROCESS

I am going to show you how to help your young athlete reach his or her goals and dreams of becoming a professional basketball player. Let that sink in for minute. I am about to give you the roadmap to high school basketball, college basketball and professional basketball. Big promise, but you are going to become a believer as you keep reading. Are you ready to learn how others have landed college scholarships and professional basketball careers for themselves and their kids? Are you ready to understand how to navigate the new AAU landscape with success? Are you ready to stop feeling helpless and unknowledgeable about how to help your kid achieve their basketball dreams? If you said "yes" to any or all of these questions, you have picked up the right book. I am going to share all of the answers and solutions to your problems in the pages that follow. In this book, I am going to teach you EVERYTHNG that you'd better know about AAU basketball and how to help your young athlete turn their love of basketball into a college and eventually pro career.

No matter where you are in your basketball journey, you need to read this book in its entirety before you or your young basketball player take one more step down the AAU yellow brick road. The game has changed, and many parents, coaches, and players are still operating based on the old model. Why you ask? Well, it's because the old model is not that old. When I say not that old, I'm talking about as little as 12-13 years old. This is about the age of many of your student athletes. Heck, many of the players in the NBA today found their way to success during the era of the old AAU model. So, there's no surprise that they still abide by the old rules. It worked for them. The only problem is that it won't work for you.

However, don't worry. I am going to show you how to choose the right AAU team for your young basketball player, how to make sure that your kid is mastering the right skills, how to put your kid on the path for a great high school career, and how to make sure that he or she in the perfect position for a D1 scholarship and eventually a pro career.

WHERE'S THE PROOF?

How can I promise all of this? Well, over the past year, my son Moses and I have interviewed over 40 different basketball pros. We interviewed NBA vets, D1 College coaches, top-ranked players, their parents, top AAU coaches, and industry leaders, and we discovered something. We discovered a path towards having a successful basketball career. When we started this interview process, I was hoping to uncover a path to the NBA. Like many of you, I had no clue as to what we needed to do or how we should do it. So, I went in search of a clear series of steps that anyone could take to increase their chances of making it to the league or to playing professionally overseas. I had a hypothesis that becoming a professional basketball player was as navigable as becoming a doctor or a lawyer, and what I discovered is that I was right.

After uncovering what seemed to be a path to the answers to all of my questions, I couldn't believe that no one had put together a "How to Be a Basketball Pro" Handbook. There is a school, or a handbook, for how to succeed in pretty much any and every profession that you want to pursue. But we couldn't find one for basketball players. So, we did what most AAU basketball parents do. We started our own team!

JUST KIDDING! (Thought about it, but just wanted to focus on helping my kiddo.)

No…I did something else. I went out in search of the information and put the handbook together myself. After multiple talks with our interviewees, the path to success began to reveal itself to us. We could see where some missed a step in their journey causing them to go in a different direction, and most importantly, we were able to see where others chose the right step and were able to achieve their dreams because of it.

We then reverse engineered their tales of middle school, high school, college, and professional basketball and found that there are multiple commonalities in all of their journeys. We found what we were looking for. We found the basketball yellow brick road, we started to follow it, and it started to work! We were blown away. It was like discovering King Tut's tomb. We wanted to make sure that we did everything to the letter and secured our path towards our next step even more, so we started to study our findings and wrote down every detail.

It was obvious that we were onto something. Seeing our success, other parents started asking us for the keys to the city of AAU, and I started sharing with them what I had found through our research. Well, some of it. The rest I put in this book.

However, it's funny how when other people start to ask what you are doing, it adds validity to your ideals. So, we went back to double check our findings to make sure that we knew what we knew and we found out that we did. We also found some gems that we had overlooked

We sifted through the 40 plus interviews with a fine-toothed comb, and in a matter of months, the roadmap to becoming a professional basketball player went from a map atlas-type overview to a GPS. I am confident that this book will give you an in-depth look into our findings. My hope is that this book will also help you and your kiddo become one of the few that turn their passion for basketball into a basketball career. So, sit back, relax, and take in our discoveries. Turn off all possible distractions my friends. You are not going to want to miss this information. Your young athlete's career depends on it.

As a keeper and now sharer of this knowledge, I must tell you that not everyone is ready for this information, so share at your own discretion. In the world of AAU, you are going to become a "round-earther" amidst a community of "flat-earthers". Pun intended. For those of you who don't get my little joke, Google "Kyrie Irving flat earth". All joking aside, let's get one thing clear before you read on. If thousands of non-NBA playing parents can get their kids to the league, you can, too. The first thing that you have to do is realize and accept the fact that it is possible.

"It's not who you think you are that holds you back. It's who you think you're not." - Anonymous

THE PROOF IS IN THE PUDDING

Now, Moses makes every team that he tries out for. Imagine what it will be like when you send your kid to AAU basketball team tryouts, as a formality, because you already know that she or he will make the team. Imagine what it will it be like when you and your young player change your post-game in-car discussions from "How many points did you score?" to "Did you reach your written goal for the game today?" Imagine what it will it be like when your kid walks onto the floor during the game and the coach of the opposite team calls out, "shooter," as the ball is about to be inbounded to him or her.

Imagine what it will be like when you go out-of-state or to showcase camps, and your kid grabs the attention of college and top high school coaches? Do you have a picture of that image with you and your smiling player? We do, too. You see, that is our life right now, and if you do the things that I am suggesting that you do in the book, this will be your reality as well.

Now, instead of wondering if he is going to make the team, we talk about if we want to play for the organization. We ask ourselves if the team is a good fit for our son's future goals. We ask ourselves if the system being taught is a good fit for our son's playing style. We ask if this team is something that will help him on the next step in his process. Instead of hoping to get a roster spot, we ask, "Is this situation good for what we want to do?" It's different and very empowering; I wish this feeling for every parent and player out there. You deserve to feel that feeling and my mission is to make sure that you get to.

Now, instead of saying how can we score 10, 15, or 20 points, we say things like, "Today, we are going to work on finishing, and the next game, we are going to work on one dribble pull-ups. The next game we are going to work on steals, and the next game, we are going to work on blocks" and so on. We have used the tools and tips that I am going to share with you to move our son from working on ability to working on mastery.

Now, our conversations include discussions about how to do better at the next level. There isn't a concern about if we will get to the next level. The focus now is mastery. We do this so that when he gets to the next level, he can excel. It's quite different.

We have had pro basketball players notice his game and elevated play, and we know this because they have walked up to us and told us as much. We have had college coaches' notice his play, and some of them have even come up to talk to us about how much they admired his hustle and love for the game. They also talk to me about his proficiency in scoring and ball handling. It's a wonderful way of being and it's possible for you and your young athlete as well!

Now that you are filled with sunshine and rainbows, let me share a few of the mental blocks that we as parents and coaches like to create on our young player's journey. You will probably encounter them as well, so it's important that I make you aware of them. This way, they don't blindside you like they did us, and this way you can remove them from your experience as quickly as they arrive.

CHAPTER 4. DON'T THINK YOUR KID'S DREAM AWAY

The problem is that most people THINK that they CAN'T do this. They operate within the old paradigm, and then fail and say to the basketball community, "See, I told you it was hard." They say things like, "You better not get your hopes up. The percentage of people who make it is .000001 percent." Instead of working to be that .000001 percent, they give up. Making them and their young athlete the "rest." You see, one of the biggest problems that you will face will be the uninformed masses.

They will try to direct you and your young player as you go down your basketball journey. The only problem is that they will be directing you in the wrong direction. They will direct you towards multiple dead ends, and they will do it with conviction and a fervent passion. Their enthusiasm and vigor will be a protective camouflage for their uninformed wrongness, and because you are new to the game, they will condemn you for your new fact-based beliefs. Most of the time, they will be doing it out of love and true concern, while other times they will be doing it as a means of sabotage. Yes, unfortunately in the world of AAU basketball, much like the world of business, some are out to see you fail. (Actually most are out to see you fail. I was trying to be a little more positive, but I figured that for your benefit, it's best to keep it real).

The coaches of the past system will say things like, "You just have to be born with "it," or "If you stop growing you won't make it." Other coaches will say, "You have a better chance of winning the lottery than playing in the NBA," or "You have to play on the same team for years in order to get a chemistry going. It's essential." Lastly, you may hear, "Working out with trainers is a waste of money." And the list goes on and on. Just for fun, email me some of your favorites. I would LOVE to hear them. You can reach me at info@hoopchalk.com. I will respond.

As your young athlete's skill level grows you will encounter parents who will yell some non-kid friendly things at your child while he or she is playing. You will have fellow team parents withhold information about opportunities in order to secure a better spot for their children. You will have jealous detractors at every turn. You will have people who will try to impose their doubts and self-sabotage onto you and your young athlete. As you move closer and closer to your goals, the crowd of detractors and their opinions and suggestions will grow larger and louder. It is then that you must grow tighter and more closely knit as a family, or as a mentor and player.

If you are going to succeed, you MUST take on an "us first" mentality. You must always do what is best for your family and what is best for your young athlete, point blank and period. Do not get caught up in making emotional decisions any longer. You must approach this journey with the pragmatism of a Jeff Bezos and the emotional disconnect of a Steve Jobs. Your child's future depends on it. You are about to enter into the basketball colloquialism zone. You will encounter the "You have to be born with it" colloquialism roadblock. You will encounter the "You have to be tall to play basketball at the next level" roadblock. You will encounter the "You have a better chance of winning the lottery than playing in the NBA" roadblock.

However, what many basketball guys and gals don't know is that those colloquialisms, and their accompanying friends, are utter bollox. Let's break them down one-by-one with facts, instead of emotional, good old basketball head talk. If you are ready for the mind shift and the ridicule that will come with it read on. If not just skip to chapter 5. It's cool either way. There is still a lot of value in knowing the information without having the mental shift that the next few pages are going to give some readers. Either way you have been warned.

BASKETBALL MYTHS DEBUNKED
(<<<READ AT YOUR OWN RISK>>>)

Read the following pages at your own risk. You are approaching the point of no return. Once you have this information, you will become an outlier. You will open yourself up to ridicule and possible community banishment. After reading the following paragraphs, you will become the innovator/risk taker of your city and possibly your state. This might sound exciting, but innovators are not appreciated by the "establishment," so reader beware. Innovators are seen as trouble-makers and dreamers. Read on if you wish, but be aware that you have been warned.

Most people don't like new information, whether it is fact-based or not. Remember, round-Earth believers were once burned alive, and scientists where burned at the stake and ostracized. Countless others who dared to challenge the status quo have met worse fates than those. You don't have to read on. If you would like to stay a little safer, just skip this section and continue reading in Chapter five. (Final Warning!).

<<<<<<<< MYTH BUSTING DANGER ZONE>>>>>>>

For those of you still with us…welcome. You are about to become the Billy Beane of your local AAU Basketball community. I guess by default that makes me your Peter Brand. I'm cool with that. Welcome to the 1 percenters. Your ideas will be mocked and criticized, but your athletes will begin to separate themselves from their peers. Welcome to the world of the game changers. Are you ready? Let's get started. As mentioned before in the safe section, here are the factual, often discarded, arguments against the age-old ideals of youth basketball.

Myth #1 – "You Have To Be Born With It."

Many of you know of the late starter stories in basketball. You've read the stories of athletes, like Michael Jordan, who got cut from his high school team. You've probably watched the stories retold by Steph Curry on how he had zero college offers, and last but not least, you've probably heard about how Russell Westbrook wasn't even on anyone's radar until his senior year. All of these players were born with one thing and it obviously wasn't an "it" factor. The thing that they were born with was the desire to work harder than everyone else.

Very few, with Steph Curry and Kobe Bryant being the exception, NBA stars have NBA star offspring. With a league chocked full of talented ball players, how is it that hardly any of their "born with it" genes get passed down? I mean, if you look hard, you might be able to find 5 NBA players whose children went on to be superstars, but even that would take some deep research and probably would lead to a fruitless search.

No, the "Born With it" factor doesn't exist. The worked for it factor does. Just ask Kobe, LeBron, Larry Bird, Magic Johnson, Steph Curry, Kevin Durant, and Michael Jordan. All of these superstars credit their abilities to hard work. It's the obvious elephant in the room. However, because it sounds more anecdotal and "folki-taley" people keep talking about the "born with it" gene. Hey it's easier to explain why many don't make it. It feels better to say that I just wasn't born with it. It stings to say, "I didn't work hard enough for my dream." Like it or not, the latter is the reality and the former isn't. So commit to doing the work that others won't.

Myth #2 – "If You Stop Growing, You Won't Make It."

I have three words for people who say these words to young athletes and they are Allen Iverson, Spud Web, Isaiah Canaan, Jameer Nelson, Aaron Brooks, D.J. Augustin, Darren Collison, Kyle Lowry, Kemba Walker, Aaron Brooks, Patty Mills, Peyton Silva, Raymond Felton, Trey Burke, Will Bynum, Phil Pressey, John Lucas III, Earl Boykins, Nate Robinson, Jameer Nelson, J.J. Barea, Isaiah Thomas, Ty Lawson, Kyle Lowry, and Chris Paul. Okay, that was more than three words, but you get my point. The best part is that Chris Paul, at 6 feet tall, is among the tallest of the group. Not to mention that if you look at the ESPN Top 100, you will find that quite a surprising number of them are 6 feet and under.

How is it that all of these "height challenged" basketball players got to play in the highest levels of the game? Some of them even played for 10-15 years in the league. I would say that it's because the game is a lot simpler than many would like for you to believe. As Steve Smith of Oak Hill High School says, **"The game is about who puts the ball in the hole the most during the game. That's it."**

The basket doesn't care how tall you are. The ball doesn't care about your shoe size. The basket only cares about how well and how often you can reunite it with the basketball during the game. Here is what Earl Boykins said in our interview:

(Earl Boykins Interview On Hoopchalk Basketball Podcast) - 14:12)

Moses: What was it like to play in the NBA?

Earl Boykins: What was it like to play in the NBA?...I...Mose...it's...that's a hard question. Because when you're playing in the NBA, it's all you know. You don't know anything else. You don't know anything else as...you know it was great playing on television. You grow up... you know I remember being your age, Mo, and at the time, you know you would see all of these guys playing on TV. The TNT games, and CBS and ABC games, and your like, you want to play at that level and to finally make it, to finally walk into a NBA locker room and see your name on the back of an NBA jersey it's like WOW!

I can remember going, pulling up to arenas, and when you see a kid your age, Mo, with a Boykins jersey on. It's like...man, this is real! It's real. It's real, so...It's hard to even explain after playing in it. It's hard to explain because it's like the ultimate. It is the ultimate.

Me: That is amazing man. Well, let me ask you this question because I, I don't talk about this much. But, I was able to do some stuff through acting and Broadway and stuff like that, and a lot of people along the way always tell you, "It's impossible", "you can't because of this", "you can't because of that". It's like, you're not good enough for this, you are not good enough for that. What would you say to those young players out there who feel in their soul that they are meant to do this at a higher level, but may not have the people around them to say, "Hey you can do this, just put in your work and go out there and do your stuff. You can do the things that you want to do." What would you tell them? The ones that are hearing this podcast.

Earl Boykins: I think the first thing I always tell kids when I see some..., especially the short kids like me. The first thing I tell them is: Number 1 - you have to be realistic.

Me: Uhmmm.

Earl Boykins: By that, I mean that you have to realize the things that you are going to have to overcome. I knew that because of my height that I had to be a better shooter than another guard. Because if I wasn't, that was going to be held against me.

Me: Right.

Earl Boykins: I had to be a better ball handler than another guard because if I wasn't, that was going to be held against me.

Moses: Right…

Earl Boykins: I had to be quicker than the other guard because it was all going to be held against you.

Me: Right.

Earl Boykins: And…once you realize at a young age, o.k., these are things that are going to be held against you, because of my height, because of my size. It's much easier to have the belief that you're gonna play Division I basketball and Division II, NBA, overseas. Because I can remember being younger than Moses. I remember when I was in the fifth grade; I actually believed in my heart that I could shoot better than Larry Bird.

Me: YESS!!!

Earl Boykins: I actually believed in my heart that I could shoot a basketball better than Larry Bird.

Me: Yes!

Earl Boykins: I always had an unbelievable self-confidence in myself. I always had an unbelievable self-confidence in myself. When I was in the NBA, and you look across the court and you're going to be going against a Kobe Bryant.

Me: Right?

Earl Boykins: An Allen Iverson, a Gary Payton, a LeBron James. You're going up against these guys and my mindset was always, "I'm going to be better than you on this night."

Me: Right! Right!

Earl Boykins: This night, right here, I'm going the best player on the court. I don't care about the other nights, but this particular night, I'm going to be the best player.

Me: Right!

Earl Boykins: And I always believed that I was the best player on the floor.

You can take a listen to NBA Vet Earl Boykins tell you the whole thing himself at aaubasketballbible.com

Myth #3 – "You Have A Better Chance Of Winning The Lottery Than Playing In The NBA."

In the past, it is very probable that going to the NBA could have been about hitting the lottery. It was the Wild, Wild West back then. It was definitely about being in the right place, at the right time, and finding the four-leaf clover of basketball court gods. No, that is not a nod to the Celtics.

Lakers all the way baby! However, with the infusion of money and shoe deals, all of that has changed. Now, the pathway to the NBA is hidden in plain sight, and anyone who knows where to look for it can find it. Take Lavar Ball for instance. His son, Lonzo, didn't play for a high level "shoe brand" team. He didn't find the magical "born with it" gene because Lavar never played in the NBA. He (Lonzo) just had a father who found out one of the factors that help young players "make it." Actually, he found many of them, but we are only going to talk about one as it relates to this myth.

That factor is awareness. The new lottery ticket is knowing what gyms to be in and what teams to be playing against. The new lottery is on-court and off-court awareness. Win or lose, if you are not in the right gym, you are drastically decreasing your odds of success. Work on this and it's like buying a bunch of lottery tickets. Awareness is an odds multiplier.

Myth #4 – "If You Are Good, You Will Get Discovered."

If you believe this, I have some ocean front property in Arizona that I'd like to sell you. (Love that old country song by the way.). I would encourage you to take a listen to one of our first interviews. It was with a dear friend and basketball liaison for a small basketball prep school in Kentucky: Coach Q. Coach Q told us of a friend of his who coaches for an NAIA school, who had an average of 300 emails a day from new prospects wanting to go to his school. All of whom were 6'2 – 7' feet tall; all of whom could jump out of the gym and all of whom had touted amazing double digit scoring stats. Do you mean to tell me that all of them were not good enough to be "discovered?"

"C'mon MAN!" – Chris Carter

Every pro knows of a guy who was better than him, who didn't make it to the league. EVERY ONE of them can name him even today. So, how is it that all of those guys didn't get "discovered"? How is it that the ole anecdotal saying of "be good and people will find you" skipped ALL of them? Maybe it is because, as Lavar discovered, the saying **IS NOT TRUE**. The new game is attention and being findable. The new game is finding the scouts, playing in front of them often, and making your own fortune, as Michael Schwartz said about how he helped his son D'Shawn become ranked #69 in the country by ESPN.

(Michael Schwartz Interview - 24:50)

Moses: D'Shawn talked about getting on a circuit team or on the right team. So, how do parents find out about circuit teams that are near them and how important do you think that was as a parent looking back at D'Shawn's journey?

Michael Schwartz: I could talk about this for the rest of the day. I mean, I think it's super important and something you have to consider if you have an elite player. You know for a long time, I wasn't aware of the difference being in

Colorado Springs. I thought it was all hype; I didn't understand that being on a circuit not only provided exposure, but it's also exclusive meaning. It doesn't matter how good you are or how good your team is; the coaches attending those circuit events won't see you unless you're on the Under Armor, Nike, or Adidas team, and I never knew that so that's big because we were a great team, but where it's exclusive, we can't get in. So, why is that important to parents from a logistics standpoint; you know, you only have a certain amount of viewing periods a year that a kid can be seen, and a college only has so many coaches that go on the road.

Me: Right.

Michael Schwartz: So, they want to get the biggest bang for their buck. They'll go to an EYBL tournament, see the best players playing the best players, and you know the majority of the kids that they've heard about; that's where they're at.

Me: Right, right…

Michael Schwartz: So, they'll jump from an EYBL to a Under Armor to an Adidas. They'll usually play in the same area to make it easier for coaches, so why would a coach take an extra flight you know unless he's recruiting somebody specific? He's gonna hang out there and see, ya know, as many kids as he can versus going to some corn field somewhere and sticking his head in a gym seeing what he can see you know? Um, but, I was prompted to put D on a circuit two hours before we actually, or two years before we actually did, and I didn't listen. I, I hadn't witnessed the difference until we went out with the Colorado Hawks during early viewing period. You know, you have to educate yourself and see what's available to you in the state and um, ya know, what kids have benefited, um, and if possible, ask the kids that have supposedly benefited to make sure it's true because a lot of them will just name drop and have a great sales pitch, you know as far as the organizations and stuff.

But, um, I would tell you, in my opinion, the program in this state that has the most to offer would probably be the Hawks. Billups is a great program and so is Colorado Chaos, but we did, we did play for several in state organizations, but D wound up meeting L.J. from KC Run GMC at USA Junior National Camp Actually. L.J. inquired about him and D happened to have just left the team he was with prior, so he was kinda like a free agent and after speaking with a lot of people and comparing, you know, it kinda went K.C. Run; that entire experience was top notch for sure. You know, a lot of people might say, "Well, you know D knew he wanted to go to Colorado;" anyway, pretty much already had it, but you know, with recruitment, you'll find out you can never count your eggs until they hatch.

Me: Right…Right…Right.

Michael Schwartz: And even if that was the case, we felt it was just as crucial to get as much experience as he could playing with and against the best players in the nation on a regular basis, in order to give him the best swing at preparing for college level play. Because you know regular season of AAU; you'll see one team you'll beat 'em, you'll probably beat the second one, and then the third one will be a struggle, the fourth one'll beat ya.

Me: Right.

Michael Schwartz: On circuits, every game is a battle.

Me: Nice….

Michael Schwartz: There are no blowout games. You know, but…

Me: That's great.

Michael Schwartz: But, you know as far as other states, um, you have options being in Colorado because seven states touch us. You know, in Oklahoma, you got Oklahoma Run PWD, which is Under Armor, it's extension of KC Run; you have team Griffin, in Oklahoma, that's EYBL sponsored by Jordan; KC Run Being in Kansas. You know Phoenix Family in Arizona; there's a lot.

Me: Ok.

Michael Schwartz: Um, and a lot to research, but you know again, being in Colorado you know, you just have to do your homework and it's important to remember not every kid can play on a circuit or needs to be on a circuit, you know.

Me: Right...Right...Right...

Michael Schwartz: You have to be realistic with yourself, too. Look at the team; ask yourself will my kid even play on this team. Because it could be a great team, but a bad fit if that makes sense, you know.

Me: Right, Oh, yeah. Yeah. Yeah.

Michael Schwartz: So, you don't want to waste your time and money, you know, pursuing some circuit team that your kid isn't going to showcase what he can do on, but I mean it's possible to get heard about in other ways via high school, word of mouth, and smaller programs. But, you gotta know being in Colorado, it's automatically gonna be harder being in Colorado Springs, even harder than that.

Me: Right...Right...Right.

Michael Schwartz: We just don't have the opportunity other states have, and you know all I can say is face every decision on an educated, you know, research process with the intent of giving your kid the best opportunity you can.

Me: Definitely, definitely. You know it's funny you say that because I mean, and maybe there's some truth to it, but I keep hearing just be good and people will find you. But, I was like that can't be the answer. For me, I was like you have to put yourself in a good situation and hearing you say that is kinda confirmation from what I was thinking.

Michael Schwartz: Well, yeah, and I mean and there are those stories of people that you know that they never did anything, they never went anywhere, and somebody just heard about 'em and found because he was good. But, you know, with what I do for a living, you know, I don't know much about basketball, but I do know marketing and you need two things for marketing. You need a good product and you need potential buyers to put it in front of. And, you're going to get a lot more success by putting him in front of more potential buyers than maybe three or four.

To hear the complete interview go to aaubasketballbible.com

<<<<<<<<<Now Leaving Danger Zone >>>>>>

Other roadblocks that you will encounter include the loss of friendship, the dissemination of wrong information, and possibly being ostracized. However, remember that once you start to play club/circuit basketball, you have decided to enter the business part of the game as well. As one of my mentors used to say, "It's not show friends; it's show business." Understanding this helped me navigate my music career and turn it into a record deal, and even a stint on Broadway. Imagine what understanding this fact can and will do for your young athlete.

The reason most people fail at this basketball thing is that they are winging it. They don't have a system to guide them to where they want to go. Many basketball parents and families are relying on other people to guide their future and their child's future. As my momma used to say, "Everybody ain't your friend, baby." - Katie Horne.

Truer words were never spoken. The only person who will have your best interest at heart, 100 percent of the time, is YOU. So, keep reading and inform yourself of the current, best practices of AAU basketball. You are about to gain access to what I believe is the best system available based on our research and over 40 interviews with the current AAU and NBA basketball minds. Well, here we go.

CHAPTER 5 – HOW DO I KNOW IF THIS STUFF WILL WORK FOR ME?

Well, full disclosure: every kid is different and every situation is different; however, there are some constants that apply to all basketball situations, and because of that, I know that these tips and tricks will work for you. This book addresses those constants and how to deal with them on your basketball journey.

Moses Winning Mr. Hustle Award At KU

Using the tips and ideas that I have shared with you and am going to share with you, has allowed Moses to make every team that he has tried out for. He has been able to build "brand" awareness in the state, and we are now moving to make him a national elite player and name. He has won many Elite Camp championships, been recognized with a Mr. Hustle Award at Kansas University's summer basketball camp, and received "Student of the Year" awards here from our local Gold Crown organization owned and operated by former Nugget Bill Hanzlik. He has won MVP awards while participating in the Rise Up Elite 8 showcase camp, and he has been nominated as a top 10 player at Ryan Silver's West Coast Elite camps. He currently plays on the top 13U team in the state. All signs point to success, and I can't wait to see what the next level is going to bring now that we have even more information.

Moses At The Elite 8 Showcase Tournament

Based on his play and brand alone, we have been able to secure interviews with Coach Smith, Jason Richardson, Earl Boykins, Ryan Silver, Chauncey Billups, Jim Huber and countless other basketball icons. We have been able to do all of this by using the information that I am going to share with you in this book. If we can do it, you can do it, and I'm going to show you how.

IT WASN'T EASY – OUR STRUGGLES

In the beginning, I struggled with all of the things that most parents new to AAU struggle with. I wanted my kid to learn the game. I wanted my kid to have fun. I wanted my kid to bond with other basketball playing kids, and…I wanted him to be an instant super-star. During the season, I wanted my kid to be on the "right team" and get lots of minutes. I wanted him to "want to win" like I wanted him to win. I wanted him to be upset when he lost. To be honest, I wanted to have a junior Kobe. However, that wasn't what I had in the beginning. I had what most of us have, and that was an 8, 9, or 10-year-old kid. A kid who liked to play basketball and that was it.

Moses was so happy playing basketball that he would often be caught dancing on the floor during free throws. He just loved to play. Win or lose, he just loved to play. As a typical AAU dad, I struggled with understanding that. Why wasn't he aggressive? Why wasn't he a killer on the court? Why wasn't he a junior Kobe? Well, part of the reason was that he was still a prepubescent kid. He had probably less than zero testosterone coursing through his veins, and he just wanted to play basketball. The fact that it felt like the games that he watched on television with a ref and a uniform were nothing but icing on the cake for him! Long story short, I wasn't trusting the process.

So, before I go any further, let me give you moms and dads reading this book a little hindsight advice. Let your kid be a kid. They aren't going to "want it" until middle school or maybe high school, and that change will happen with the introduction of testosterone and puberty. Until then, they are just babies playing a game that they love. Trust the process and give them time. They will get there.

With girl players I have found that it is important to surround them with competitive peers. Girls are different altogether. If you want your young lady to be a "dawg" on the court you are going to have to surround her with other "Dawgs." As Keiko Yoshimine of Advantage Basketball Camps said:

(Keiko Yoshimine Advantage Basketball Camp: 11:39)

Moses: So is the basketball journey different for girls than it is for boys do you think?

Coach K: I think to a certain extent it is. Um, ya know for guys I think that...maybe it's not the journey that is as different as just kind of the perception. Like, for instance, guys who are basketball players like say in high school. I feel like they are, you know, kind of like the kings of campus right?

Me: Uhmm

Coach K: The football players, basketball players um they're looked highly upon. Whereas for girls it's maybe not as much of a prestige thing to be on a sports team um for them and sometimes, in some cases, can carry some negative stereotypes. And so some girls will shy away from those opportunities just for that. And for some reason there's this thing with girls where they don't want to outshine their friends.

Me: Ahhh

Coach K: It's this really weird, Ya know just from watching from seeing how some of these girls react to success and to you know like, full on just beating somebody they kinda shy away from that and they'd rather stay with the pack a little bit more and so I think it takes a special, special type of person to overcome that fear of being ostracized or being you know kind of not really, um being part of the main crowd if you go ahead and kind of show out for that. You know?

Me: Yeah

Coach K: But you know there's actually, it's kind of a double-edged sword though because, because not as many girls are trying to play basketball um there are more scholarship opportunities.

The AAU Basketball Bible
Everything You'd Better Know About AAU Basketball

Me: Hey!

Coach K: Because of title 9 usually you have the same amount of scholarships out there. Umm so there's really more opportunities to earn a college scholarship for the number of players. You know for boys there's you know, very, a slighter number of opportunities compared to like the number of girls that play basketball

You can hear Keiko talk more about that in her own words at aaubasketball.com

Lastly, remember that you are a grown ass adult and you have gone through puberty. You have gone through the maturing process. No matter how tall they are or how good they are at the sport of basketball, always remember that they are still a kid, and for the most part, they are playing to please you. They aren't the Mamba yet, and they aren't supposed to be. You can start planting "Mamba seeds" here and there, but always be aware that you are talking to a baby.

Around 13, you will notice the "Mamba seeds" starting to sprout and then you can give them a little fertilizer with the "Mamba talks" and extra drills. But, until then, treat them like they are a "Baby Mamba," and let them enjoy the game.

But wait! There's more.

The AAU Basketball Bible
Everything You'd Better Know About AAU Basketball

In the beginning, aside from trying to bring out the inner Kobe in my 8-year-old, I ran into some other AAU common roadblocks. Some of the universal roadblocks include other AAU parents, over-promising coaches, having my son put into the paint because he was one of the taller kids, my own self-doubt about my lack of knowledge of the game, and the laundry list of other stuff. I ran into the "daddy ball" politics and the horrible referees. I ran into the personal trainers and the crazy sideline parents. If you can think of it, I ran into it. We diligently checked off all of the AAU roadblocks in the beginning. I was a bit of a parental wreck during those days, so it shouldn't have been a surprise when those doubts and fears started making their appearance in my young player. Some of the things that we struggled with in the beginning were:

- On-court confidence.

- In-game minutes.

- Trying to find the right AAU team.

- Learning that AAU/Club basketball wasn't enough and that we needed to be on a circuit team.

- Trying to navigate bad team situations. (One of our coaches actually got into a physical fight with another coach in practice.)

- Trying to align ourselves with the right circuit team.

•   And other things…

It was difficult and not very fun.

I remember having long car rides home after games. I remember wondering if I was doing the right thing for my kid. I remember finding the "big" programs in town and thinking that we had to be on their team to "make it." I remember trying to do everything that I could do to help my kid, and I remember feeling like I was doing it all wrong.

However, it all changed when I started using the things that I am giving you in this book. Our worries were assuaged by the wealth of knowledge that we uncovered during our podcast interviews, the many books that we read together, and the documentaries that we watched. We soaked up every after -interview conversation with college coaches, NBA vets, and college players.

We purchased online program after online program; we hired trainer after trainer, and we found out, that for the most part, no one had all of the answers that we were looking for, but they each had some of the answers.

Nobody could give us a step-by-step process to make it to where we wanted to go. It was kind of shocking to me, as a parent, until I realized that the game had literally changed a little more than 10 years ago. The new AAU was so new that no one had taken the time to reevaluate the process that they were telling us to trust. So, we continued to interview and do our research, and just like that, the path became clear.

CHAPTER 6. THE YELLOW BRICK ROAD, AND THE ROADBLOCKS

As you have seen, listened to, and read, we now travel in the circles of the people that can guide us to where we want to go on this AAU journey. Moses and I are constantly doing interviews with the top names of the basketball world, and we are now looking to guide him towards becoming a top-ranked high school player.

Everything that we have learned on this journey has helped him catch the attention of top-level icons at the next level. He has even been blessed enough to receive basketball tips from NBA legend John Lucas.

(John Lucas Interview - 19:45)

John Lucas: Moses: too upright, get lower, attack going downhill, don't settle for so many jump-shots.

Moses: Yes, Sir!

Me: Thank you so much for your time; this is absolutely amazing.

John Lucas: Thank you!

That means that he was actually watching this young man play. He was watching him enough to know something about his game, from a two-day camp with hundreds of kids. That says something about the work that we have done and the success of the exercises that we are going to share with you! Hear the entire interview here at aaubasketball.com

Moses has also received tips and direction from Mokan Elite's founder and former head coach, Jim Huber.

(Coach Jim Huber - Interview

Me: Well, you have your own podcast there at Breakthrough basketball, which is awesome, and on your show, you interview a lot of great coaches, a lot of great basketball minds. I really love listening to it, so my question to you is what one thing would you say is a win for an athlete as far as coaches go? We were talking about the intangibles, as far as making eye contact, firm handshake, saying "thank you." Is there one thing that you constantly hear from coaches that if you keep hearing that, coaches are like "that's a win for the athlete?"

Jim Huber: So, like Moses, if I was talking to you about that, I would tell you this, remember this...Everything matters, everything matters, and what I mean by that is this. How you warm-up, so before the game, how are you warming up? College coaches are watching everything. How you sit there, like in the beginning. Are you kinda communicating with your teammates getting them ready to go? Um...during the game, a bad call happens, how do you respond to it?

Me: Hmm.

Jim Huber: Do respond in a positive way? Do you hand the ball to the official? Do you run back to the other end? Are you making body limb rolls, rolling your eyes? Bad body language throwing the basketball, sliding it away from him? Coach takes you out of the game. Are you kinda walking off shrugging the coach off? Are you sprinting off? Are you telling the player subbing in for you "Hey, you got number twelve? Are you coming off slapping your teammates five? You making eye contact with the coach nodding, taking it in even if you don't want to hear it? You sprinting in to the bench getting your drink or whatever? Coming back sitting by the coach, engaged in the game, clapping for your teammates? You know, what are you doing? A bad play happens during the game. Somebody makes a bad pass; are you going to yell and scream at your teammates? Are you encouraging them saying, "That's alright; that's alright; let's play; let's go. We got this."

Me: Yeah…

Jim Huber: Kid makes a bad play; all of a sudden, he's got his head down. You coming up to him patting him on the back? "Come on man! Jim, you got this! Come on, baby, let's go!" You guys haven't made a couple stops down the floor. Are you encouraging your teammates, getting them up…"Let's go! We got this! Let's get a stop here!" Are you huddling your teammates up on a dead ball? Are you talking to your teammates? Are you being that leader? Are you being an extension of the coach? Everything matters. You lose the game and it was a tough game; are you sitting there like not wanting to shake other people's hands? Are you sitting there like a towel over your head? Is it more about you? Everything freakin' matters, man!

And when kids understand that and you need to realize too Moses. You might be in a gym playing and there might not look like there's any college's coaches in there. And I might be in the gym watching and I might know college coaches. And all of a sudden I watch you and I walk out of the gym and I call and say buddy, hey Coach Keely have you seen this kid named Moses play? Holy Cow man he's out of Denver man. He's really good. I think he could play at your level. You don't know who knows somebody that's gonna tell somebody about you. And… and…Somebody could be watching a practice. How you practice matters. Every rep you take matters. So when you take that mentality that everything you do matters. Then your gonna have an opportunity to impress somebody because their gonna see you doing all of the little things because that's who you are.

(You can hear his words of wisdom at aaubasketballbible.com

not to mention personal guidance from countless other basketball greats like Earl Boykins and Jay Humphries, former first-round draft pick and assistant coach to the Brooklyn Nets. We have truly been blessed and we are excited that we get to share all of this with you)

Moses is well on his way to achieving his dreams and your young player will be, too.

THE AAU BASKETBALL ROADBLOACKS

Oh, the basketball mental roadblocks heard around the world. A lot of people won't succeed in helping their young player reach AAU success because they will fall victim to the AAU basketball roadblocks. I know I almost did. They almost sabotaged everything. When I began this journey, I believed the basketball myths that we talked about earlier – things like "He's gotta be born with it to make it." I believed that I didn't want to have him practice too much because I didn't want to burn him out. I thought that we had to be on the top team in the state to make things happen for him. I believed that you had to be super tall to make it to the next level, be it D1 or the pros. I bought into them all. Hook, line, and sinker and they almost ruined everything.

So back to the roadblocks, which is what we are supposed to be talking about in this section. What are these basketball roadblocks that so many of us fall prey to you ask? Well, there are a lot, but I am going to share with you the ones that are near and dear to my heart. #sarcasm

These are the ones that I hear all over the gyms across America, and to be honest, they make me sad for the kids that have to hear them over and over again. If there is one cause of kids burning out or not going to the next level, these are the top basketball roadblocks that trip up countless young players and parents in the game today.

DON'T PUSH YOUR KID. THEY MIGHT BURN OUT

If your kid is "burnoutable", this is not his or her field. You both should know that before you spend countless hours and thousands of dollars in the gym. If they can get tired of playing basketball, they need to find that thing that they can't get tired of and do that. It's better to know that earlier than later. Great players don't get burned out. Could you imagine Kobe Bryant saying, "I played a lot of years in the league. I am SO burned out on basketball?" Do you think that you will ever hear Steph Curry, LeBron James, or Michael Jordan say, "If I don't ever see another basketball again, it will be too soon?" No! Because that is the one thing that they feel as if they were put on this earth to do! If your kid can be burned out, you need to let that happen while they are young, so that you can help them find the thing that they won't be burned out on.

P.S. If they think that they are burned out on basketball, tell them wait until they have to get a job. I like to tell Moses your best bet is to master this basketball thing, so that you can make basketball your job. 9 to 5 for 30-40 years vs 3-4 hours a day for the next 8 years in order to do what you love is quite a perspective shaper.

YOU HAVE TO STAY WITH THE SAME TEAM, SO THAT YOU CAN BUILD CHEMISTRY TOGETHER

As our Coach Jim Huber of Mokan Elite says, "You, Troy, can't be pressured by other parents, other coaches, and other people; you have to do what's best for your child. Cuz when someone else gets in that situation, they're gonna do what's best for their child."

Me: Thank you for saying that because you know we're in Denver; so, it's not a huge basketball place, but so many times people get caught up in exactly what you're saying and it's so good to hear someone in your position say look! It's about taking care of your kid and making sure your kid is in the best situation. Not all the other things that sometimes we get hit with in, you know, smaller markets where it's like, you know, "Hey, you gotta stay here because they've been playing together since, you know, third grade."

Jim: You're gonna get. Yeah...you know, "Don't get into that."

In our interview, Coach Huber says that the most important thing that you can do is to put your young player in the best situation for him or her and your family. Now, here's the cold hard truth that many AAU directors and coaches won't tell you. Are you ready? Read this slowly and twice on Sunday..."Most of your 12u, 13u, and 14u basketball team will not make your club ball team once you enter high school." I repeat, "Most of the kids that you played with in middle school will not make your circuit high school AAU basketball team." There, I wrote it out twice just to make sure that you read it twice and got it into your head. It's not personal; it's business.

If your kid doesn't know what their role is and they are a team player with no special contributions to the team (i.e. prolific scorer, rebounder, defender), they will not make the team. Let me clarify, they won't make the team if it is a shoe affiliated or circuit team. Shoe teams have to have winning teams on their circuit or the brand feels as if it doesn't have as good of a chance of aligning itself with a future college or NBA player.

You see, in high school, it becomes about the business of basketball. That means we need to win; point blank. Period! For the most part, teaching and developing is on you at that point, and if you haven't elevated your game by high school, you are kind of behind the 8 ball and being cut will be your barometer. All of this to say, while your kid is in middle school, you need to find the team that is going to best develop your kid. Wins in middle school don't mean ANYTHING! Why? Because most of the kids on your middle school AAU team will NOT make your high school AAU team. Did I make myself clear? Good! Now that you are aware of this, don't worry about your middle school wins. Just let your young athlete play and work on skill work. It worked for Jamal Murray. His father, Roger Murray, would only do skill work with him in middle school.

In our interview with Mano Watsa, the founder of PGC Basketball, Coach Watsa told us about how Jamal's father, Roger, would put him in club ball for a season just to see where he was skill-wise, and then take him out and work on the skill that was lacking. After they felt like he got better at that skill, maybe the following season or the season after that, he would put him back in AAU basketball to see where he was.

They did this all the way up to the 10th grade. Now, he plays for the Denver Nuggets. I guess it worked out.

(Mano Watsa Founder of PGC Basketball Interview)

Mano Watsa: You know you might be interested to know, I mentioned before we jumped on for this episode that Jamal Murray from the Denver Nuggets grew up in my home town, and interestingly enough his dad didn't allow him to play AAU basketball until he got to 10th grade. Because his dad wanted him just to focus on development not competition….

Take a listen here to our interview with Mano Watsa, where he tells the story in his own words at aaubasketballbible.com

COLLEGE ATHLETIC SCHOLARSHIPS ARE VIRTUALLY IMPOSSIBLE TO GET

If college D1 scholarships are so hard to come by, how did Lavar Ball secure three in one year? If you started making "rational" excuses about how he's different or about how he is special or about how Lonzo Ball is a special player, put this book down and don't pick it up until you believe that you have a special player, too. I'm being serious. No amount of knowledge can help you or your young athlete, if you don't believe that you have a special talent in your household. Sure, he or she might not be 6'7", but neither is Steph Curry or Chris Paul. He or she might not be super athletic, but apparently neither was Larry Bird. There are countless stories about how un-athletic and slow he was. Just watch his documentary. I think the presenter talks about his lack of athleticism in the first 30 seconds. The presenter is then followed by other NBA players who echo his sentiments about how slow and un-athletic Larry was; however, Larry Bird became an NBA legend.

Watch the video at aaubasketballbible.com

The first thing that you have to do is believe that you can secure a college scholarship for your son, daughter, or young athlete. Belief is the 1st rule of AAU basketball success, and if you don't have that, you need to put this down, leave your AAU team, and come back when you do. Belief is really that crucial. If you don't believe that it's possible, then it isn't possible. If you don't have confidence in your abilities to help your child get to the next level, how will your child have confidence in her- or himself when playing?

Getting a college scholarship is one-third ability, a third confidence, and a third awareness. By ability, I mean that you have to be able to do what you need to do on the court. By confidence, I mean that your young player has to be confident that she or he can do what's needed on the court; and your belief in your kid is a big part of that. Also, know that when you are confident, you are going to be tested and that is where the ability comes in. Finally, you need to have awareness and, by that I mean, the coaches have to know who the heck you are.

As Michael Schwartz said in our podcast episode earlier, "They have to know who you are." As D'Shawn Schwartz said in his interview…"I saw a guy get a college scholarship for diving on the floor." The problem that most parents don't grasp is the awareness concept and the awareness concept is key. With an inbox filled with hundreds of unopened emails a day, awareness is your VIP pass.

I HAVE TO BE RANKED TO GO TO THE NEXT LEVEL

Yes, being ranked matters! Do you have to be ranked to go to the next level? No. Does it help? Yes! Do you need to be ranked in middle school? No. In fact, it's almost better not to be ranked in middle school. I say that because there is a belief in the basketball community that the top 5th, 6th, 7th and 8th graders do not go on to be top-ranked high school players or even capable college players. So, why place your youngster in that position? There will be plenty of time to work on being ranked and that time starts in high school. As a friend and basketball coach of mine said to me, as we prepared for the start of our basketball journey…"Show up late."

He said, "Troy, do you remember high school dances?"

"Yes." I responded.

"Remember how everyone would be having a great time and then after the party started, a really pretty girl would walk in a little late and everyone would be talking about her?" he continued.

"Yes," I said.

"In the world of basketball, you want to be that girl. You want to be the pretty girl that shows up late. Work really hard so that you look great when you show up, but show up late," he said.

At the time, I thought, this guy doesn't know what he is talking about, but then his daughter got one of the few D1 full ride college scholarships in our state. So, maybe he knows a thing or two about a thing or two. All of this to say, rankings are good, but go after them a little later than 5th grade. (Actually a lot later.:))

Work on your game and don't think about rankings until around 10th or 11th grade.

Summary: Work hard now and show up late to the game ready to dominate.

YOU HAVE TO BE ON AN ELITE TEAM

No! Kenneth Faried didn't play on a "top team" and neither did the Ball brothers and that was in high school. In middle school, it is all about getting better. Period! In middle school, it is all about skill mastery. No, let me clarify, in high school you want to do one of two things or both. The two things that you definitely want to do in high school are…

1. Play against top competition and/or

2. Go to elite camps to play in front of college coaches against top competition, and you want to do this during the live periods. As we learned from Coach Austin Kelley, the top times to be seen by college coaches are in June and July.

(Coach Austin Kelley Hoop Group - 10:45)

Me: ….You guys have had 128 Alumni that are playing in the NBA. Karl Anthony Towns, uh, James Harden, Kevin Durant, all those guys, and um, so it's like how do parents start getting involved? How do they know which camp to put their kid in whether or not they're like, "Hey, I want to see if my kid can play against top level kids or I want to see if my kid, I want my kid to get better, or I want my kid to, you know... whatever...how do they know.

Coach Austin Kelley: Yeah, they're gonna have to understand um, you know, the summer recruiting schedule, if you want to call it that, if they're looking for the high level stuff.

Me: Uhmm.

Coach Kelley: You know, there's a thing called the NCAA live period.

Me: Right, right, right…yeah!

Coach Kelley: Yeah, so there's three weeks in July that college coaches are allowed to be out, and you know during those three, they're usually your most competitive times for the most competitive camps that we run. Those are the ones that those kids come to…to get that college exposure.

Me: Gotcha. Gotcha.

Coach Kelley: And then, and then, you know, from there we run Division II and Division III, you know, recruiting period camps, so if that's something that they're looking for understanding that schedule. You know, that's gonna be in June, or you know the spring and fall times of the year.

Me: Ok.

Coach Austin Kelley: And then other than that, you gotta understand with the July live period, a lot of things are directed and kinda formed around that.

Me: Right Right, Right

Kelly: You know a camp in July versus a camp in June. You're gonna have you know high level competition. Kids from all over the place. More's on the line for a lot of kids you know since it is that time that those schools can be out and recruit. The ones that have the scholarships to offer

Take a listen to our interview with him here where he talks about the live period. Visit aaubasketballbible.com for all of the chapter resources.

CHAPTER 7. THE AAU NEW TESTAMENT

Now that you have been baptized in some of the knowledge that we gained during our 40 interviews, let's get into the meat of the book. Let's have a little history lesson on the ever-changing world of AAU basketball. Let's start with the big change that happened in AAU ball right around 2001 or so.

In the movie "Sole Man," Sonny Vaccaro, the founder of the shoe deals, talks about how the landscape changed when he was ousted from his deal with Nike. Before leaving Nike, Sonny was the guy responsible for Nike taking over college basketball. He was the guy that took Phil Knight's little shoe company and made it the shoe of the NCAA. His idea was based on Nike's difficulty with breaking into the NBA. At the time, the NBA was dominated by Converse, if you can believe that, and getting players to switch to Nike was proving difficult for the then new brand Nike. So, Sonny in his brilliance said to Phil and the Nike executives, "Let's get them (the young college players) shoes, so that they will fall in love with the brand before the NBA. Let's get them to fall in love with Nike in college!"

How did he plan on doing that you ask? By getting the college coaches to get their teams to wear Nike shoes. How did he do that you ask? Well, at that time in college basketball, the coaches had to buy their own shoes as a part of the athletic budget. Converse was a coach's favorite because Converse, at the time, was cutting the coaches a deal on the shoes because they were buying in bulk. Sonny, knowing this and knowing that the coaches only made about $20-30k a year, (again, this was the early years), said to Nike, "Let's give the shoes to the colleges for free and on top of that pay the coaches a little something, something for the honor of giving them shoes." It was like paid advertising. The Nike executives loved this because even at $100k a year, for some of the larger schools, this was an advertising price cut. Billboards and radio cost a lot more that $100k a year. So it was a win-win situation.

Nike loved it. The college coaches loved it and, by default, the players loved it. Everyone was happy. That is until Nike fired Sonny.

Being a little angry, some might say understandably so, he decided to go work for Nike's then rival, Adidas. Adidas was not even in the basketball game and wanted to be a player. Hey, mo' money, mo' money, mo' money. They tried to get NBA players to jump ship and join the Adidas brand, but Sonny had done such a great job getting the now NBA players to love Nike that the switch, along with the lack of financial incentive from Adidas, made the move a little difficult for most.

So, Sonny being Sonny said, "Heck! Let's go younger. Let's get involved with high school players." Just like that, the Adidas ABCD camps where born and the shoe game became a high-school business. ABCD camp birthed players like Antonio McDyess, Stephon Marbury, Kobe Bryant, Rashard Lewis, LeBron James, Shaun Livingston, Josh Smith, Kevin Love, O.J. Mayo, and DeAndre Jordan to name a few. So it wasn't that long ago. The game literally made the big change in '92, but started changing the youth AAU basketball landscape around 2001 with the immergence of the King himself, LeBron James!

Later, Sonny was fired from Adidas, and the game started to trickle down into middle school. I guess they couldn't do elementary, so they stopped there for now. All of this to say that the new AAU landscape is less than 13 years old, as of the writing of this book with the last ABCD camp being held in 2006. Many of the players that made it to the league didn't have to go through the new world of AAU to get there. Many of the guys, in the current NBA, are products of the old AAU system. That's right; many of the guys in the league right now did not go through the same ins-and-outs that you will have to go through to be successful. So, here we are with a totally new set of rules and a totally new set of outcomes and possibilities.

Enter you and your kid with 20- to 30-year-old ideals and a desire for success. Do you see how that might be a problem? History lesson over. For a deeper dive, watch the

30 for 30 documentary "Sole Man." (Not the 1986 Movie with a person doing black face. How the hell did that movie get made?) See the documentary over at aaubasketballbible.com

Now that we are all caught up, let's work on helping you get where you want to go in this AAU world; the NEW world of AAU. Step 1…I know that everyone wants to know about how to best situate yourself to procure a D1 Scholarship (and some of us, the pros), but the process says that you have some steps to go through first. The first step is to train like an elite player. There is a difference. Besides as John Lucas said, at his camp in Los Angeles,

"Parents, all that your young player can do right now is go to the next grade." – John Lucas

So right now help them work on being the best player going to the next grade. How do you do that you ask? Well let me share with you what we have learned. The first step is training like an elite player. Training like an elite player will not only build your confidence, but is the hidden key to more playing time.

THE KEY TO MORE PLAYING TIME...

The AAU Basketball Bible
Everything You'd Better Know About AAU Basketball

So, you want more playing time for your kiddo. Well, the best way to do that is to train like an elite athlete, and that has more to do with quality than quantity. We learned about the difference first from Dave Hopla, the man who doesn't miss shots. I would talk about his career, but his bio does it best. Here is an excerpt from Coach Hopla's bio:

"…In 2006, Hopla was hired as a shooting consultant for the Toronto Raptors. After joining the Raptors, Toronto increased its team shooting percentage every month, from 44.2% in November 2006 to 47.5% in January 2007. They also increased their 3-point shooting percentage from 30%, in November 2006, to 40%, in January 2007. In 2007, Dave Hopla was hired by the Washington Wizards as an Assistant Coach for Player Development. His knowledge, expertise, enthusiasm, energy, passion, and love of the game are unmatched by anyone." – - davehopla.com

To put it mildly, Coach Hopla knows a thing or two about a thing or two. The first time that we heard the idea of skill mastery or elite training, we kind of heard it, but didn't hear it to be honest. That was until we heard it again in our interview with Jon Hildebrandt, aka Superhandles.

It was in our interview with Jon that we heard it by another name. He called it "Skill Mastery."

Interview With Jon Hildebrandt – Aka Superhandles

Moses: Do you have more pieces of advice that you'd like to give to parents or young players

Jon: Yeah, It would basically be to just expand a little bit on what we were just talking about with the measurement. I think that emphasizing measurable skill mastery with your son or daughter should be an emphasis instead of skill dabbling.

Me: Right

Jon: You see once you start putting numbers into your drills it becomes completely different. Instead of just drilling without a purpose you can suddenly at that point compete against yourself. So your practices can become games. So you can compete against your previous score, but in terms of what parents can do with their young players or with their son or daughter. Initially when learning here's just a little progression to go through, but if they are learning a new drill or a move, first work on it and do one.

Just get to the point to be able to do it one time and then the next goal is then two in a row and then three and eventually 10 in a row. And once at least ten in a row can be done. Then emphasize speed. So how many can be done within a given time frame. And so coordination first , speed second and then when you do that. You're able to measure how good you currently are how much you are improving and then you can really start progressing towards mastery.

Click here to hear our entire interview:
aaubasketballbible.com

So, you want to be a go-to guy for the coach? You want to get more court time, then work on skill mastery and stop skill dabbling or logging hours because someone said that you need a lot of hours. Yes, you do need a lot of hours, but you need a lot of elite mastery hours. Here is what we like to call "Step 1."

STEP 1: ELITE TRAINING/SKILL MASTERY!

Shooting 500 shots is outdated. Yes…you read that right; JUST shooting 500 shots is outdated. That was a great tactic in pre-shoe team AAU, but in the AAU game of today, mastery is more important.

Here's why:

1.   Because of the politics that are associated with youth sports, your young player might get only 4-5 minutes to earn playing time. That means that the lackadaisical 500 shots practice will not help. You need mastery, and mastery means measuring. Measuring means knowing your numbers. You need to know your numbers. So, if you want to stick with the 500 shots, that's totally fine, but don't be upset when you don't get the results that you are looking for. What the pros and basketball mentors are

saying is…measure your makes. Measure everything.
Know your numbers/percentages.

Moses Reaching 1500 Hourse in 5th Grade

Example of Elite Training/Skill Mastery: How to practice
500 Shots from the 5 practice points on the floor for
mastery.

The AAU Basketball Bible
Everything You'd Better Know About AAU Basketball

Corner Mid-Range – 25/50: Congratulations, your player is 50% from the corner. They should now know that if they miss one from the corner in the game, the next one is definitely going in. It's just math. It's not a hot hand or cold hand; it's math. Your shoot-around practice should be aimed at raising that percentage.

Extended Elbow Mid-Range – 30/50: Congratulations, your player is 60% from the extended elbow. They should live there. They should take every shot they can there because odds are that it's going in. At least 3 out of 5 shots will go in. That's guaranteed playing time for your young player.

Free Throw Line Extended - Three Pointer – 40/50: Congratulations, your player is 80% from the free throw line extended/three-point line. Don't ever shoot anywhere else! You are about to be called "shooter" by the opposite team's coach!!

Knowing your numbers in practice will make you a skill master on the court. It will also allow you to be a go-to player in the games. It's also a confidence builder for your young player. In addition to shooting measurements, measure how many successful clean crossovers your young player can do in a minute. The more perfectly executed crossovers in a minute the better. Measure EVERYTHING! From now on, train like an elite player and know your numbers; the change in your game will be mind-blowing, and your game time will shoot up!

STEP 2: PLAY REC AS WELL AS AAU.

In middle and elementary school everything doesn't need to be competitive. Playing against normal players is great practice and it builds confidence. It gives your player a chance to try their skills and moves out on real defenders. Cones are nice, but cones don't play defense. Now, a lot of coaches will say that playing against rec league talent is a bad thing. They will argue that the things that your young player can do on rec player defenders won't work against high-level players. Only part of this is true.

The moves that you do on rec player defenders won't work AT FIRST on AAU players, but after you practice them with a live defender, you will see that eventually they will. Here is how it has played out for us in the past:

Stage 1: Moses tries move on rec player. It works! - Confidence up!

Stage 2: Moses tries move on AAU player. It doesn't work. - Confidence down a little.

Stage 3: We implement Elite Practice Techniques – We measure how many times he can successfully do the move in a minute or specific period of time. Number increases with practice.

Stage 4: Moses tries move on rec player. It works even better! Confidence up!

Stage 5: Moses tries move on AAU player. IT WORKS! Confidence through the roof!

The thing that you have to remember about every NBA player is that they all talk about the fun that they had playing in the backyard with their brothers and sisters (Reggie Miller) or the countless games spent just playing at the playground (Jason Richardson). Today's kids don't really go out and play at the playground for hours any more. Rec ball is the best way to recreate that experience for them. Yeah, it's more structured than many of us would like, but that is what we've got. So, instead of running away from it, use it as their playground time.

Give it a shot and see how it transforms your player's game. Use this method with your young player and watch their game transform. "You're welcome" (In my best Maui Voice).

STEP 3: PRACTICE MORE, NOT LESS

The process is a marathon not a sprint. Almost every elite player became an elite player "later" in their basketball career. That is because the work or the process has a compounding effect. It doesn't happen overnight. As Kobe Bryant says in his Ted Talk interview with Behind the NBA,

The AAU Basketball Bible
Everything You'd Better Know About AAU Basketball

"If I practice 4 times a day and you practice 2 times a day, eventually I will begin to separate myself." - Kobe Bryant

Take a listen to the talk in its entirety by clicking here
aaubasketballbible.com

The same is not only true for Kobe; the same is true for everyone. Everyone includes your young athlete. I know, I know, you just said 500 shots is no longer good and more time is not the answer. Now, you are saying practice more not less. What is it? Well, it's a little bit of both. You want more elite level practices and workouts and by that I mean more workouts that involve measured exercises and more focused objectives. If you are there to work on your finishing game, do elite practice that just focuses on finishing. If you are there to work on ball handling, do a ball handling workout, measure it, and leave the gym. The key to more playing time (when it counts, which is later in their basketball career or in high school) is more practice. To be clear, more ELITE practice.

"Hard work beats talent when talent fails to work hard." – Kevin Durant

CHAPTER 8: THE BOOK OF CHOOSING THE RIGHT TEAM

We struggled with this dilemma for years. That was until we learned how the whole AAU team thing actually works. My hope for you is that the following information helps you realize your power as a parent. I hope you claim that power and use it to direct your young athlete's career towards their dreams and future success. The thing that you must realize is that you actually have more power than you know as a parent, and yes, this AAU world is a game of power plays. You must know how to play the game, but most importantly you must know that there is a game.

The game is as follows. 15U and up AAU coaches, high school coaches, and college coaches want to win. No matter how much you are told otherwise, the truth is that they not only want to win; they need to win. If a team doesn't have a star player or doesn't win games in their circuit, they will lose their sponsorship with their shoe team of choice. I've seen it happen and as you go through your journey, you will see it, too. If a high school or college coach doesn't guide their team to a winning record, they lose their job. After middle school, the game is about winning. So before high school, your mindset should be - let me reframe - your mindset BETTER be about skill development.

In high school, coaches want to play players who they believe will give them a better chance at winning. In 15U and up, AAU Coaches need to play the players that will give them the best chance at keeping their sponsorship. In college and in high school coaches have to play the players that will get them further down the championship road than they did last year, or they will find themselves looking for employment. Your player is the answer to the "How do I keep my job?" question. Never forget that.

So, what does this have to do with choosing the right team? A lot! In middle school, the right team is the team that will help your young athlete get better. It doesn't matter if you lose EVERY GAME. Your team needs to help your young player get better and that is all that a middle school AAU team needs to do for you. I get it. As parents, we get caught up in playing for the best team in the state. We get caught up in 5th, 6th, and 7th grade rankings. I get it. It sounds impressive for the non-basketball world of which you were recently a part. It feels good to say to your friends my kid plays on the top 4th, 5th, 6th, or 7th grade team in the state or even the nation. However, you have to put your proud parent ego aside and do what is best for your child in the long run, and very rarely does that mean playing on a top middle school basketball team.

The right move for your young player, for the long run, is the team that makes your kid better. Find a team that helps your kid get better. Find a coach that is going to help you help your kid get better. That is your job in middle school. Get Better! Did I say "get better" enough times? No? In middle school your job is just to get better!

WHAT THE RIGHT TEAM LOOKS LIKE.

As we have discussed earlier in this book, the best move is the best situation for your young athlete. What does that look like? That looks like the team that he or she can get the most minutes on the floor with. The team that allows her or him to play needs to be your choice for now. It doesn't matter if it's the C, D, or E team. Your young player needs to play and work on in-game performance. In middle school, your job is to get better. I hope that I said that enough. Not to win, not to be ranked in middle school; your job is to get better.

So, find and watch teams and tryout for teams that will help you do that. Don't be afraid to leave a situation that isn't what you want for your young player. As Michael Schwartz said in our interview, "If the other kids find a better situation, they are going to do what is best for them. You need to do what is best for your kid." I'm paraphrasing, but you get the point.

Here are some questions that you should ask yourself when choosing to stay on a team or to leave a team.

Top 7 Questions All Middle School AAU Parents Must Ask In Order To Choose The Right Middle School Team.

Step 1: Does my kiddo play a good amount of minutes? Yes or No

Step 2: Do the other players help my kid get better? Yes or No

Step 3: Does my young player enjoy the players on his team? Yes or No

Step 4: Is the organization supportive and development focused? Yes or No

Step 5: Is the organization organized? Yes or No (This one is for your sanity.)

Step 6: Does the coach focus on skill development? Yes or No

Step 7: Does this system fit the way that my kid plays? Yes or No

Those are the top questions to ask yourself when choosing a middle school team for your young player. Things change a bit when you are choosing a team for your high schooler, but if you get 5 out of 7 yeses from these questions, you are probably in a good place. Any less than that, you might want to think about making a change.

The following are questions that you need to ask yourself before choosing a team for your high school athlete.

Top 7 Questions All 14/U AAU And High School Athlete Parents Must Ask.

Step 1: Does my young player get a good amount of minutes on the floor?

Step 2: Is the team a team with high visibility? (i.e. plays on a circuit or plays against high level teams who play on a circuit.) *AAU Only Yes or No

Step 3: What is the track record of program alumni? Do they go on to play in college or pro at an acceptable percentage? (Suggested 20-30% achieve the goal that you desire via the program.)

Step 4: Is the system good for the way my kid plays basketball?

Step 5: Is it a Daddy-ball situation. Yes or No – (If yes, the team should be removed from your list. You can't afford to do this at the higher levels.)

Step 6: Does the coach of the team have a relationship with the college coaches of the schools that I would like for my young player to attend? Yes or No

Step 7: Is it a good mental situation for my young player?

Same rule applies here. If five out of seven are a yes, then you are in a good place. If not, you might want to consider looking elsewhere for your high school career. On to mental toughness!

CHAPTER 9. THE BOOK OF MENTAL TOUGHNESS

The Book of Mental Training is a critical book. It's actually the most important, and I would suggest that you read this this part of the book over and over again. This is the most important training that you can provide for your young player. Mental training is the one thing that nobody works on and everyone needs. Do you ever wonder why so many top draft picks never pan out in the NBA? Do you ever wonder why so many top ranked high school players don't go on to excel in college? Do you ever wonder why so many top 7th and 8th graders don't go on to become top high school ball players?

The answer is mental toughness. They haven't trained their minds for the game of basketball at the next level. A lot of people like to believe that you have to be born with mental toughness, and that you have to have an inner mental drive. However, like everything else, mental toughness can be taught. Remember the TED talk interview with Kobe? Confidence can be acquired and the inner motor can be manufactured on the assembly line of mental training. Moses and I have put together a mental training program to help parents and young players with their mental training. For more information on the program, visit aaubasketballbible.com and start your mental training journey today!

For those of you not in a place where you can go to the home page of the mental training program, let me tell you a story that demonstrates the importance of mental toughness. As the story goes, it is said that Michael Jordan, in an attempt to toughen up the then #1 draft pick Kwame Brown, decided to expose him to a bit of tough love before playing with him on the Wizards. He did this in hopes of preparing his teammate for his idea of the NBA. Michael invited the young man to his house to workout together. Later in practice, at the Wizard's facility, Michael began to berate the young man with insults and trash talk. You see, Michael was using the tough love that had allowed him to become a mentally tough player; however, Kwame wasn't prepared for the mental training mastery course that Michael Jordan was beginning to teach.

As the story goes, Kwame was so mentally torn up by the interaction that he soon left the Wizards opting out of a 30 million dollar deal and decided to try his hand elsewhere. He bounced around the league for the next 12 years or so, never really realizing his full potential and was waived by the 76ers without ever playing a game for the organization. By all means, Kwame had achieved the ultimate success in the world of basketball. He had made it to the NBA.

So what happened? Why did he not dominate the league as expected by the organizations that drafted and traded for him? It seemed as if every one of the teams that he was signed to was just waiting for Kwame to become the Kwame that the world knew that he could be. So why did that moment never come? Did Kwame somehow lose his physical ability to dominate players on the basketball court? Did his skill dip? Was the NBA talent so above what he was used to that he just couldn't compete at that level? The answer to all of these questions is NO.

Kwame had a 30-point game with the Wizards and then later averaged 12.3 points and 9.1 rebounds and started every game for the Lakers in the playoffs. The physical ability was there. The only thing that wasn't there was his mental ability. Based on some of his quotes to the media, it is almost certain that Kwame never trained his mind. Don't allow your kid to become the Kwame of AAU. Here are some training tips as to how you can avoid that fate for your young player.

Read and use them as often as you do mental training. Want to get even better at helping your young athlete with mental toughness? If you said yes, go to aaubasketballbible.com and learn more about our mental toughness course. Now let's go to the "how to" of our mental training. Of course this is going to be an overview because we can't go as in depth as we would like in an ebook, but this will definitely give you a great head start.

Step 1: Write Out Your Goals And Objectives.

There is nothing like knowing where you are going. When I work out with a trainer or a workout partner, it is a lot easier to do the exercise when I know how many reps I'm going to do or how long we will be doing the exercise. Just doing push-ups or bench presses or squats until, whenever, is very difficult to do. You have no destination. You have to have a goal. Playing the game like this is also mentally exhausting for young players. They don't know what the objective is. There is no way to measure if they were successful as an individual or not. Sure, the team won or the team lost, but how can they measure if their performance was up to par or not? Well, writing out game goals will help them. Help them by writing out the goals and objectives for their games, workouts or whatever things they are doing for their betterment and basketball development.

Example: Today, I want you to score 6 points and have 2 rebounds and possibly 1 steal. That is our goal. Once you reach that goal, you can play or do whatever you want on the court.

This builds confidence and focus in your young player's mind, and it's scientifically proven to work. One of my favorite motivational speakers, Zig Ziglar, says that writing your goals down increases your ability to achieve the goal by an average of 80%. It only takes a few minutes and the results are immeasurable as far as confidence building goes.

In his story about becoming a D1 basketball player D'Shawn Schwartz talks about how he wrote down his goals in the 7th grade. He wrote that he wanted to be pursued by Pac-12 schools and he was. As of the writing of this book, D'Shawn plays for CU under a full ride basketball scholarship. He was also ranked #69 in the country and was pursued by Pac-12 schools. Write down your goals and write them down now!

Here are some things to make sure that you do when writing your goals down. I like to call this my goal template checklist. Make sure that you take these steps when you write down your goals.

STEP 2: MAKE BIG GOALS

DO…NOT…MAKE…REALISTIC…GOALS!

As Will Smith says, "You can have ANYTHING that you want. All you have to do is decide." If you have a chance to write down anything that you want, and if you know that by writing your goal down, you increase your chance of achieving that goal by 80%, why would you chose something boring and realistic? You are limitless. Don't be your own dream blocker.

The AAU Basketball Bible
Everything You'd Better Know About AAU Basketball

Write down what Grant Cardone calls "Big Hairy Audacious Goals." Write down goals that get you excited every day. Write down goals that keep you up at night. Be bold! My personal theory as to why most NBA draft picks never reach their full potential after being drafted is that their goals were not big enough. Crazy isn't it? Think about it this way.

Most players' goals are to make it to the NBA. Many basketball players don't have a goal list after the goal of "Make it to the NBA." So, when they make it to the NBA, their goal achieving, as far as their subconscious mind is concerned, is complete. They did it. Job done. Goal reached. However, once they get there, they then have to set new goals and that is a little tougher after you do all of the work to reach the first big goals. So, how do you overcome that obstacle?

Write down big goals and write down goals that you want to achieve during all points of your middle school, high school, college or EuroLeague, and NBA career. Heck, even write down what you do after your NBA career, if playing in the NBA is your goal. Write it all out and then write down the goals that you will achieve once you have made it to the NBA. Things like win three titles, two MVPs, make the all-star team. Whatever your goals are for your career after you join the league. Write them down! You can write anything that you want. Be sure to aim high.

"People do not fail in life because they aim too high and miss. They fail in life, because they aim too low and hit."
(Unknown)

STEP 3: VISUALIZE YOUR SUCCESS!

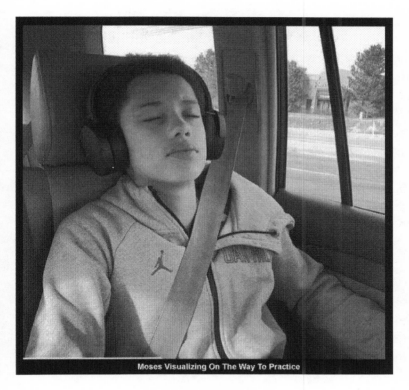

Moses Visualizing On The Way To Practice

See yourself as a winner. See yourself as a success. Arguably one of the greatest soccer players in the world talks about how he would visualize before every game. He talks about how he would play through the entire game in his mind before ever setting foot on the pitch. Pelé got to the locker room early and found a quiet space to play the movie of the game in his mind. Michael Jordan once said, "I always take and make the last shot in my mind before I ever take a shot on the court."

Golf great Tiger Woods, Aaron Gordon, Kobe Bryant and many other pros use visualization as a technique to increase their confidence and performance during the game. The gift that your player has now as a young player is that they can begin to build their visualization muscle years, and in some cases decades, before other pros did. Imagine how much of a master they will be by the time they reach their age. Start today working on their visualization game. It will be well worth it and the results are amazing.

STEP 4: CHANGE YOUR LANGUAGE

As many people discovered many years ago with the movie "The Secret" and today with various other celebrities, like Will Smith, The Rock, and Lavar Ball there is a massive amount of power in your words. You should now know that your words are very powerful things. The thoughts-are-things movement has been taken to new heights. Why? Because, it actually freakin' works! Be a proactive practitioner and apply this new knowledge to the way that you talk to you players, your kids and yourself.

We can't cover all of the how-tos in this book, but the overview is to begin saying only what you want to happen. For instance, instead of saying, "Don't miss your layups," reframe your demand to "make your layups." Instead of saying don't just stand there, say "move without the ball." Instead of saying, "You're not playing aggressively enough." Say, "Play more aggressively!" Instead of saying, "It's really hard to make it to the NBA, begin to say, "It's going to be fun seeing you on the Lakers." You get the idea. Begin saying what you want to happen and stop saying what you don't want to happen. Capiche? Good! Now let's keep this thing going. Next up, Kobe's favorite. Meditation. Here is how you do the meditation thing.

STEP 5. MEDIATE

Meditation is a great way to work on clearing your mind and increasing your focus. It is a way to help your young athlete learn to lock-in during the game. Do you find that your player is distractible on the court? Do you find that they have a hard time staying in the game? Do you find that your young player has a hard time quieting his or her mind during free throws? Meditation is the answer and it is working for us! Tell your young athlete to work on mental toughness, by working on mediation.

Now, a lot of times when I say this, people think about guys in long robes sitting by a water feature , ringing some chimes or bells or something. But that is not what I'm talking about. I'm just talking about 5-10 minutes before a game or during the day, when you turn all electronics off and just sit in the quiet of your home. No moving, no talking, no music in the background; just silence for five minutes. Kobe Bryant says that he works on his mediation practice every day. He says that if he doesn't meditate in the morning, his day is almost certain to be shot. Mediation, he says, grounds him and puts him in control of his day.

Want to know how the Black Mamba stays focused? Start doing what he does. Strengthen your meditation practice. Soon, you'll be staring through your Matt Barnes.

Take a listen to him say it in his own words.

"I meditate every day. I do it in the mornings for about 10-15 minutes. I think it's important because it sets me up for the rest of the day."
– Kobe Bryant

STEP 6: GUARD YOUR DREAMS LIKE YOU DO THE BASKETBALL

The AAU Basketball Bible
Everything You'd Better Know About AAU Basketball

As a parent, you will hear all of the statistics. You will hear all of the probabilities and you will hear all of the impossibilities. Your job is to guard your young athlete's mind from them. There is no benefit in being "realistic." The world is wide open for unrealistic people. From now on, tell your young athlete that they are going to the NBA, college, or the Euroleague, or whatever your goal is. Say it with the confidence to end all confidence.

Say it as if there isn't anything that can stop your kid from doing so. Don't let anyone else tell your player the odds or statistics on how many make it. I always tell Moses that I love it when I hear people say that only 1 percent make it and that it's pretty much impossible. Why? Because they are taking out the competition for us. If most of the world believes that it's impossible, they leave the door wide open for the 1 percent that believe that it's possible. There is your 1 percent! The one percent are the ones that believe. Here are a few examples of unrealistic people taking over the world:

Steve Jobs – Steve dropped out of college to start a computer company in his parent's garage. His little computer company became a world leader in personal computing. When he started his company, he and Steve Wozniak where buying parts from Hewlett Packard, the then dominant force in computing. Can you imagine the probability of a college dropout starting a world changing computer company in his parent's garage?

How about Venus and Serena Williams?

Richard Williams – Richard was not a tennis pro or even a tennis player. So, his kids couldn't inherit his "born with it" tennis playing genes. They had to do what our other superstars did. They had to work harder than everyone else. As the story goes, he didn't even know anything about tennis, and those are his own words. When he was interviewed, he told a reporter for Maclean's the following.

Take a look at this excerpt from their interview:

Q: When you decided all those years ago on tennis, had you considered any other sports?

A: No, because I didn't know at that time of anything in sports that a woman could do and earn that type of income. I didn't know nothing about tennis. I hadn't even watched a tennis match. I just saw [tennis commentator] Bud Collins say to [Romanian tennis player] Virginia Ruzici, "$40,000 is not bad for four days' work." I thought, that has to be a joke. But, the next day, when I read it in the sports pages, I said, "I'm going to have me two kids and put them in tennis." To this day, I don't know anything a child could do to make that kind of money in one week.

He just decided one day that he was going to have two kids and put them in tennis. He just decided this: before they were even born? Imagine the odds on that.

And last, but not least: Russell Wilson.

Russell Wilson – Russell Wilson is the quarterback for the Seattle Seahawks. Before he won his first Super Bowl, before he won a high school state championship for his high school, Richmond Collegiate School, before he was even drafted to play in the NFL, Russell's father, Harrison Wilson III, would say to his son, "Why Not You?" Imagine the odds of a 5'11", two-sport athlete, not only being drafted to by the Orioles out of high school for baseball (which he turned down), but then later being drafted by the Colorado Rockies. Imagine the odds of that same athlete later being drafted by the Seattle Seahawks. Imagine the odds of the third-round draft pick, 5'11" quarterback then taking his team to the NFL and winning the Super Bowl with a win over the Denver Broncos.

Each of these athletes and thousands more like them can tell you stories of doubters. They can tell you of the countless statistics that were recited to them throughout their childhoods. Know that you are on the right path when the doubters and statisticians approach you and your young athlete. The trick for you is to fortify your young athlete mentally with mental training. You MUST begin mental training as a part of your athlete's process.

There is so much more to this, but we have go to get on with the show. Again, if you are looking to really increase your player's mental toughness muscle join us on gameready. See you there!

www.Hoopchalk.com

*"If mental training works for the elite pros
that we mentioned before 'Why Not You?'"*
– Troy Horne

CHAPTER 10. THE BOOK OF SUMMER
CAMPS AND RECRUITING

Incoming Freshman Moses At John Lucas Elite Camp

The AAU Basketball Bible
Everything You'd Better Know About AAU Basketball

This is one of the most overlooked and misunderstood parts of a young player's basketball journey. Summer camps are often seen as recreational or just low-key instructional events. Did you know that there are summer camps where actual college coaches come to scout talent? Did you know that there are basketball summer camps where kids get scholarships to colleges and even basketball prep schools? There are also camps where kids get ranked and break out into the ESPN scene, based on their play.

That is how D'Shawn Schwartz caught the attention of ESPN. He was attending the West Coast Elite Camp in Denver. I am sure that he isn't the only one out there who can tout having this experience.

So how do you do more of the latter and less of the former? First, you have to know what some of the camps are that offer this type of exposure. The best way to determine this is to look at the camp graduate list and look at the dates of the camps. Live camps or camps that are best for exposure are the ones that are held in June or July. The ones held in June tend to be targeting D2 and D3 coaches whereas the ones in July tend to target D1 coaches.

Take a listen to our interview with Austin Kelley from Hoop Group Basketball Camp over at aaubasketballbible.com

The AAU Basketball Bible
Everything You'd Better Know About AAU Basketball

In this interview, he talks about how playing for your AAU or circuit team isn't enough. He also talks about the different live periods (times of year that college coaches are scouting players) and some of the players who have used this information and these camps to help them reach their goals. Players like Kyrie Irving, Kevin Durant, Sue Bird, Michael Kidd-Gilchrist, R.J. Barrett, and many more. It is important that summer camps are also seen as and used as an opportunity for exposure and skill check.

For a lot of players, summer camps are the recruiting key that they need. Do you have a plan for your basketball summer camp tour?

Here is a list of camps that we recommend that you put on your radar.

Middle School Basketball Camps Include:

1.   John Lucas Camp

2.   Oak Hill Basketball Camp

3.   Advantage Basketball Camps

4.   CP3 Middle School Combine

5.   PGC Basketball Camps

6.   MADE Hoops Camp

The AAU Basketball Bible
Everything You'd Better Know About AAU Basketball

High School Basketball Camps Include:

1.   John Lucas Camp

2.   Hoop Group Basketball Camp

3.   West Coast Elite Ryan Silver

4.   IMG Basketball Camp

5.   The Phenom Hoop Report

6.   Position specific shoe brand camps.

If you don't have a plan and you have a middle school basketball player, you have time. I would suggest going to visit these camps just to get the lay of the land. It's always good to know what the level of player is out there in the world of youth basketball, and camps are a great way to do it. You now have a list of the ones that you need to attend and at what stage in your career you need to attend them, so make your schedule and start traveling.

CHAPTER 11: THE BOOK OF SOCIAL MEDIA

This one can be tricky. I say tricky because, as a parent, you will now be working in a new world of sports marketing. Yes, building your kid's online social media profile is marketing and yes, you are running a business if you are entering into the game of AAU or circuit basketball. If you are longing for the good old days when you just played basketball, you are going to be left behind. I know it sounds blunt and not so fuzzy, but we don't have time to waste with the ineffective niceties. The good news is that you don't have to be a beast on all platforms. You can pick just one or two, but you definitely have to pick and begin.

Without going into a full breakdown of every social media platform, let me give you my suggestions on where you should build your child's basketball brand.

The three viable options, as they stand today, are Facebook, Instagram, and Twitter, not necessarily in that order. Here is what I have learned about the coaching community and where they reside primarily.

Instagram: Instagram is great for building brand recognition for your athlete, as far as the actual basketball community goes. You will find that your Instagram account is a great way to make your young athlete a valid player in the AAU game, as far as other players and other trainers go. This is the actual basketball community's hang out spot, so you want to be here.

Twitter: For some reason, the coaches LOVE Twitter. They live on that thing. So be advised that when they will tell you about their social media prowess, they really mean their Twitter prowess. Use your Twitter account to help coaches find out more about what you and your young athlete are doing. They won't really be looking on Instagram.

Facebook: Facebook is great for the coaches that you have a personal connection with. Once you have made it into their inner circle, you can connect with them on the "Book of Face." Prior to that, you will probably have trouble connecting with industry leaders here. Most of the coaches and scouts see Facebook as their family-time private space, so be advised.

TikTok: Tiktok as of the writing of this book is the new social media platform baby. Nobody knows exactly what to do with it, but everyone seems to be dancing and doing short videos on it. My suggestion to your young athlete and you is to hop on and just look around. Have them post a video or two and make most of them about some kind of basketball trend. Not all of them need to be about basketball but the idea is that you will be established once we figure out what the heck we are doing with the platform.

The wrap up is this:

- Instagram = Youth Basketball Community
- Facebook = Personal Space
- Twitter = Basketball Business
- TikTok = Just Build Who Knows What's Going On Here

Keep this in mind and you should be good for now.

CHAPTER 12: THE BOOK OF RELATIONSHIPS - IT'S GOOD TO BE SEEN

As I said earlier, I am a musician by trade. I have been blessed to perform on Broadway and television; I have toured the world performing my music for crowds all over the planet. Blah, Blah, Blah… The other day, I walked onto a stage where I hadn't been performing for a while, and the smiles on the faces were really great to see. One of my fellow musicians said to me, "It's good to see you, Troy." My response was the usual, "It's good to see you, too." To which he responded…

"It's Good To Be Seen."

There is a community just like that inside the basketball world. Your job is to become a part of it. The tricky part is how. I am going to show you how to do it the right way. Aren't you glad that you picked up this book? Making your way into the inner circles of the basketball decision-makers is just like entering any other inner circle. You have to enter with an intent of goodwill. That is the #1 must in building a relationship with anyone anywhere. You have to be in it for what you can give and not what you can get.

By being a giver first, you will always be welcome. You have to be a person that elicits a response like, "It's good to see you." And that only happens when you enter the relationship from a space of giving. So how do you do that the right way?

The first step is knowing who you are and what you offer to the community or relationship. If you are a great marketer, offer your services as a marketer. If you are a great fundraiser, offer your services as a fundraiser. If you are a great networker, offer your services as a community connector for the organization. Now, I know a lot of you will be thinking to yourself, "I don't do any of those things; I don't have anything to offer. That's NOT true, but let's go with that idea. Let's say that you feel like you don't have anything to offer.

First, I would suggest that you look at what your young athlete provides and see what basketball organization her or his talents are the best fit for. Your giving could be the missing piece of that team's puzzle. Every team has an upcoming spot on their roster. Your job is to see if that spot is a fit for what your child offers. For instance, if you notice that a team has a point guard that plays similarly to the way your child plays, then it's time to "do the math."

The math is recognizing if that student's graduation will line up with your student's enrollment. For instance, will that player be a senior when your child would be enrolling as a freshman or will the current young player be a sophomore? If the answer is a sophomore, then it's not a good fit. Find another team with a player similar to yours and find one that has that player graduating or entering his or her senior year around the same time that your child will be enrolling. Make sense? Good.

Once you have found that fit, do your due diligence on whether that student's success is an outlier or if the school has a history of graduating great players at that position. If this is a pattern for the school (i.e. they graduate a lot of great guards, centers, forwards, or whatever your young player is, that go to the next level), then see if the organization offers a summer or an elite camp. Your first visit should be to get to know the campus, school, or university to see if it is a good fit for your family. I would suggest going twice, at a minimum, to make sure that you like the place.

If all goes well and you feel as if this could be a great place for your child, then introduce yourself to the staff and inquire on the steps to being a part of the organization. You will probably be the only person who has been there multiple years in a row, and if your young athlete has come to the camp using the tactics in our Gameready course, she or he will be a camp stand-out anyway. Now you will be putting your family in a position to offer something that the organization needs. If you have properly done your scouting, you will know that. Here are some things to check off before considering and organization.

• The organization currently has a star player who provides a similar skill set as your young player.

• The organization has a track record of helping students with a similar skill set as your player reach their goals.

• The organization, campus, coaching staff, etc. is a good fit for your family and for your young athlete.

• The organization will need a player with a similar skill set to continue running their system.

• Your athlete's skill set is a fit for the way that the organization plays basketball.

If all of those are a fit, you have the basis for a mutually beneficial relationship, which has a strong possibility of leading toward success for your young athlete's goals. Now, it's time to inquire about the enrollment or team tryout process, preferably both. The relationship building is something at which most people fail because they approach it in one of two ways.

1. **What can I get out of this?** This is how most people come into the world of AAU. This is also why coaches are so guarded and stand-offish. Now to be clear, you should be getting something from every situation that you enter into, but you should be looking to offer back just as much as you are getting. One-way streets only work downtown and even there, they aren't well traveled. Make sure that you are entering into every situation with the thought of what can I give to this relationship.

2. **I just want to show up and have someone work it out for me and my kid.** This is the fastest way to getting blindsided. Your kid's career is always, I repeat, always your responsibility. You should never leave your player's career or destiny up to someone else. Take control, seek knowledge, and most importantly, apply the knowledge

that you gain. Your role is "mommager" or "daddager" of a future college athlete or NBA star.

"Know your role and do your job!" – Dwayne "The Rock" Johnson

My suggestion is to do the following. Learn everything that you can about the process. Pick up every book that you can. Watch every documentary that you can and listen to every podcast that you can. Do your homework and be willing to invest in your kid's career. Don't try to get a D1 Scholarship or NBA career on the cheap. As John Lucas said to all of the campers who attended his L.A. John Lucas Camp...

"Some parents complain about spending 500 to 1,000 dollars a month for training, camps, and AAU trips. I don't think that's enough. You are trying to make your young athlete competitive against other athletes for a full-ride college scholarship. That's easily 150-200k. Some of you want to compete for a multi-million dollar NBA contract. In my opinion, a thousand dollars a month for a chance at a multi-million dollar contract is not enough." – John Lucas

I think that he might be onto something.

CHAPTER 13. THE BOOK OF COLLEGE SCHOLARSHIPS

Ahh, the wonderful world of college sports. Playing in college seems to be the big goal of most AAU team players. However, I'm sure that for many of the parents reading this book, college is a goal on the way to the bigger goal. Either way, it is definitely something that you want to know how to navigate. The big question seems to be how to do that successfully. Well, here is the answer.

Here is what we have seen thus far based on the kids that get college scholarships at major universities. As I read over the outline for this section, I'm noticing that it's kind of an overview of all of the tips that we have talked about in this book, but it's always good to recap.

STEP 1: WORK HARDER THAN EVERYONE ELSE AND BECOME SKILLED.

This step cannot be skipped. Everyone likes to go straight for the reward and who wouldn't, but the key to the reward is work harder than everyone else. Train more than everyone else. Have a private coach, parent, or trainer that helps you fine tune your skills. Buy basketball training programs, watch YouTube videos on basketball, and watch documentaries on your favorite basketball players. Know more mentally about the game and work harder than anyone else. This is the key to success in basketball and in any field. Work harder than everyone else and work on mastery, not just logging hours.

STEP 2: GET GOOD AT ONE THING.

I know that everyone talks about being a well-rounded player, but that is the quickest way to zero offers. If you are going to take a roster spot, the coach needs to know which one to put you in. Are you a great point guard who can create for him or herself and can finish around the rim? Are you a tenacious rim protector? Are you a lights out three-point shooter? Are you a lock-down defender? What spot are you going to take? What need are you going to fill? You have to know that and you have to focus on being the best in your region at doing that one thing.

STEP 3: FAMILIARIZE YOURSELF WITH THE COACHING STAFF OF COLLEGE TEAMS THAT YOU WOULD LIKE TO PLAY WITH.

A lot of parents of kids say things like, "I want my child to get a D1 scholarship." But, like our guest Jim Huber said on our interview with him, "What does that mean?" Does that mean high mid-major? Does that mean mid-major? Does that mean low mid-major? What does going D1 mean? Get specific down to the school that you would like to attend. Know what each of the different levels mean. Be specific and focus on what you want. Do NOT generalize!

STEP 4: MAKE SURE THAT THE SYSTEM AND THE COACH FITS YOUR SKILL SET.

Most players will say things like, "I'm a 6'4" athletic guard, but I can play the wing, or the point. Well, thanks for making your dream coaches job even harder. The last thing that he wants to do is figure out where to put you, especially when he has three hundred emails in his inbox daily filled with kids who know exactly what they do. Well, not all of them. Most of them will be saying things like, "I'm a 6'5" guard and I can do it all." So here is the deal.

College coaches don't need players that can do it all. They need players that play their way and fit into their system. I know that you think that you are the next Jordan, but they don't need that right now. They need someone who will play well and produce within the constructs of their current system. It is your job to find out if that is you. So, watch a game, or three, or nine, or a couple of seasons, and know if the school that you apply to plays in a way that serves your skillset best. This will allow you to not only know if the school is a good fit; it will also allow you to serve the school.

STEP 5: SIGN UP FOR THEIR BASKETBALL RECRUITING LETTERS ON THEIR WEBSITE.

This is something that I didn't know about until our interview with Coach Q. You can go to the actual website of the schools that you would like to attend and fill out their prospective student athlete form. So, Google "Prospective Student Athlete Form" for your school and fill out the form. It's that simple. So, go do it….NOW! The big schools don't have this. (I looked. No for UK or Duke or…) However, read Step 6 for information on how to get on their radar.

STEP 6: GO TO THE REAL DEAL CAMPS (NOT THE NON-REAL DEAL CAMPS).

It's always hard to know what camp is good for your young athlete, and you might have a wasted camp experience or two. But that is just the way that it goes. To make it easier for you, we did an interview with a few of the Real Deal Camps and I will list their names below. Seeing as how this is an eBook, I will be updating this list as we go along, but as it stands, the two that I can see that are great camps for college coaches are as follows.

Hoop Group (June and July Camps): As we learned from our interview with Coach Austin Kelley from Hoop Group, once you get into high school, you want to be attending camps in July and June depending on if you feel as if your athlete is a D1, D2, or D3 athlete. Hoop Group has based their summer camps and camp dates to fall within the live period. If you have questions about the live period and when they fall, be sure to listen to our interviews with Austin Kelly and Coach Steve Smith. You can find them both on our podcast website at hoopchalk.com.

John Lucas Camps – ALL OF THEM: This was one of the best camps ever for Moses. There were scouts there that we had read about prior to going to the camp and probably a few that we hadn't read about. This is a low-key, real deal opportunity to get on the world radar for college basketball.

West Coast Elite: (June, July, and Academic School Camps are their thing): This is the camp that D'Shawn Schwartz went to that put him on the map with ESPN. So, there is a one-on-one relationship to success. My suggestion to you would be to make sure that you pay attention to live period times and that you select your camp based on the live period, if your intent is to be seen by college coaches. Ryan Silver was very kind to talk about the camps on our podcast. I would like to close this section with something that he says in our podcast that was really life-changing.

(Ryan Silver West Coast Elite Interview 18:20)

The AAU Basketball Bible
Everything You'd Better Know About AAU Basketball

Me: What one piece of advice would you give to young players coming up right now would you say?

Ryan Silver: I would just say patience. You know a lot of people want everything right now. And this is a, I call it a roaring river; it's a long journey and there's a lot of ups and downs, and things are not always going to go your way. But, if you're patient and you work hard, things will eventually work out.

If you would like to hear his thoughts on the live period and academic camps, be sure to visit our website to hear the interview in its entirety.

Also, ask your coach to refer you to shoe brand camps. That is, if you play on a circuit team. Adidas, Nike, and Under Armor all have position camps that are for the elite players on their specific brand teams. Ask your coach about them. If you don't play for a circuit team find out if there is a circuit team near you that you can get on. You don't have to be on a circuit team to make it to the next level (i.e. college or the pros), but from what I have seen, it definitely helps.

And finally…

Hoop Phenom Report-This camp was gifted to us by Coach Steve Smith. He mentioned it specifically when asked about camps that he might suggest kids attend for high-level competition and exposure. Be sure that check these camps out. You won't be sorry.

CHAPTER 14: TIPS FOR SUCCESS

Well, we have come to the end of the road and I can't let go (in my best "Boyz II Men" singing voice). No, but seriously. Without going back through all of the stuff that I have already beaten you over the head with, let me give you a few closing tips for success that I think will help you going forward.

Tip 1: Read and reread this book. Come back to it often. We will be changing things as we learn new information. That is the beautiful thing about eBooks. They can be living documents and this book will definitely be that. So read, highlight if you are on Kindle, and bookmark. You can also share, but make sure that you hold on tight to your own copy.

Tip 2: Write down your goals and have your young athlete do the same. YOU MUST DO THIS! If you don't do anything else, make sure that you and your young athlete write down your goals. Your next week goals, your next month goals, your next year goals, and then your life goals. Whatever you do, write it all down and read it often.

Tip 3: Find a group of supportive parents and players on your journey. Make sure that they have the same destination in mind. For instance, if the group's intention is to get ranked in high school and your intention is to go to college, then the group isn't a good fit for you. If the intent is to get college paid for and your intent is to go to the Euroleague, then the group isn't a good fit for you. If the group's intent is to go to the Euroleague and your intent is to go to the NBA, then the group isn't a good fit for you. Are you getting the idea? Either way, join a group of like-minded people and allow them to share their experiences and their journey with you and you with them.

Tip 4: Take care of your kid and yourself FIRST! As Michael Schwartz said, in our interview, it is very important that you look out for number one. This is a business and if the shoe were on the other foot, the other person would do the same. No personal or emotional attachments as Jim Huber said. Make sure that you are finding the best situation for your family and your young athlete. PERIOD.

Tip 5: Be a constant learner! Never stop learning. Watch documentaries, read books, and research articles. Most importantly, ask questions, ask questions, and ask questions!

If you are ready to take your young athlete's career to the next level and you don't know how to do it, there are a few great options to do so. See our resources section at the end of this book for more details.

CHAPTER 15: SO WHAT SHOULD I DO NOW?

Here are some options and action steps that you can take now.

Option 1: is a free option: Subscribe to our podcast! You should do that anyway, if you haven't already. Every week, we talk about the world of AAU and the new happenings in the world of youth basketball. You can find us on any podcasting platform by searching **Hoopchalk Basketball Podcast**. We are literally everywhere, and if you can't find us, send me an email and I will make sure that we are on your favorite podcasting site A.S.A.P. We are all in this together.

Option 2 : You can also like and follow our page, if you just want to read our findings. You can do that by clicking here: https://www.facebook.com/hoopchalkbasketballpodcast/.

We are here to help.

Option 3 is for the Super-Serious, Future NBA Parents: If you are ready to join us and help your child be one of the few that make it to the NBA, you are going to want to join our mastermind program over at Gameready.com. Over there, we talk about the mental part of the game that is often overlooked by young players. If you are going to the league, then you are going to want to join this group.

Click here to take our Gameready course: http://gamereadycourse.com/.

Well my friends, we have actually come to the end of the road here. If you have any questions, just reach out to us. At this point, you have all of the information that you are ever going to need as far as the next step goes, and if you feel like there is something that we missed or that we didn't discuss, just send us an email, or contact us on Facebook, Hoopchalk.com, or contact us on our website aaubasketballbible.com There literally is no excuse for not having the information that you need.

If we know it, we will share it with you, and if we don't know it, we will find it out and share it with you. Thanks again for taking time out of your day to learn about the world of youth basketball with us. I know that this has been a path-changing time and we look forward to being a part of your journey going forward.

In closing, I will leave you with this. Always believe in yourself and believe in the possible. Everything is possible. And in the words of Harrison Wilson (Russell Wilson's Father) -

"Someone has to win the Super Bowl, Russell. Why not you?" To you, I say…"Someone has to go the NBA. Why not You?" See you on Draft Night.

ABOUT THE AUTHOR

TROY HORNE is a dad who knew nothing about the sport of basketball except that his son wanted to grow up to play the sport professionally. As a former professional musician, Broadway star and television actor he had a hypothesis. That hypothesis was that there were certain truths that held fast in all professional industries. He believed that the staples of work hard, master your skills, meet the right people, and put yourself in the right places were not only essential for the music business, but essential for all professions. So he went in search of the information that he thought that he would need to help his son Moses reach his goals and dreams. *The AAU Basketball Bible* is a collection of that research. His hope is that this book can be a resource for parents and coaches like him who want to help their children or young athletes reach their goals. Troy loves educating and inspiring others to succeed and live the life of their dreams. This is a part of that work.

Learn more about the Hoopchalk AAU Basketball Podcast here: http://hoopchalk.com/

The AAU Basketball Bible
Everything You'd Better Know About AAU Basketball

Other Books that you might enjoy include:

The AAU Basketball Bible Interviews:

**Mental Toughness For Young Athletes (Parent's Guide)
Learn more by clicking here: https://amzn.to/3emmOoV**

**Mental Toughness For Young Athletes (Young Athlete's
Version) Learn more by clicking here:
https://amzn.to/2yj8mxK**

The AAU Basketball Bible
Everything You'd Better Know About AAU Basketball

Learn as we learn by joining us on Facebook here:
http://bit.ly/HoopchalkFB

Make sure to check out our mental toughness training
course for young players and coaches here:
http://gamereadycourse.com/

**Click here and get all of your FREE DOWNLOADS and
book resources!** http://aaubasketballbible.com/

For Questions and Interviews About The Book Contact Us At :
info@hoopchalk.com

The AAU Basketball Bible
Everything You'd Better Know About AAU Basketball

Links to the Interviewers Organizations mentioned in the book:

Basketball Summer Camps

John Lucas Basketball Camps:
https://johnlucasenterprises.com/camps

Ryan Silver – West Coast Elite Basketball Camps:
https://www.westcoastelitebasketball.com/

Austin Kelley Hoop Group: http://www.hoopgroup.com/

Mano Watsa PGC Basketball: https://pgcbasketball.com/

Jim Huber Breakthrough Basketball:
https://www.breakthroughbasketball.com/

Earl Boykins Boykins Basketball Academy:
http://boykinsbasketball.com/

Keiko Yoshimine Advantage Baskeball Camps:
https://www.advantagebasketball.com/home.htm

M.A.D.E Hoops Basketball Camps
https://www.madehoops.com/camps

Phenom Hoop Report: https://phenomhoopreport.com/

CP3 Middle School Combine: https://www.cp3nmsc.com/

The AAU Basketball Bible
Everything You'd Better Know About AAU Basketball

Michael Schwartz Design Company:
https://www.facebook.com/halodezign/

The AAU Basketball Bible
Everything You'd Better Know About AAU Basketball

ONE LAST THING...

If you enjoyed this book or found it useful I'd be very grateful if you'd post a short review on Amazon. Your support really does make a difference and I read all the reviews personally so I can get your feedback and make this book even better.

If you'd like to leave a review then all you need to do is click the review link on this book's page on Amazon.

Thanks again for your support!

Made in the USA
Columbia, SC
30 January 2024

31172621R00079

The youth basketball scene has changed. If you are not up to d.
with how things work today, you are going to be left behind. Do
be left behind! Don't leave your kid's future up to old informati
and guesswork. Take the reigns! Want to help your young pla
have a better chance at reaching their dream of playing at the n
level? No matter what that is for you and your family, this book
help you reach your next destination.

This book is chock-full of informat
from over 40 interviews with bask
ball industry leaders, coaches, p
and vets. If you are serious abc
helping your young basketball pla
successfully navigate the world
youth basketball, high school bask
ball, college recruiting and the life
a pro basketball player, you want
read this book.

Moses Horne is a 13 year old basketball
player at the time of this writing. His contributions to this book include working out at
the gym in order to get better and being a
little annoying to his father during podcast
interviews. I love you, son!

THE AAU
BASKETBALL BIBLE
.com

"There's that moment every morning when you
look in the mirror and ask yourself are you committed or are you not?" - **LeBron James**

$12.9
ISBN 978-0-692-13110-
5129

9 780692 131107